S0-BLV-951

TOUCHING CHINA

"Close Encounters of the Christian Kind"

Gospel Operation International
FOR CHINESE CHRISTIAN

Other books by Leona Choy

(Authored, edited, or collaborated.
Foreign language translations noted)

A Call To The Church From Wang Mingdao
Andrew Murray, Apostle Of Abiding Love
      Spanish, Dutch, Chinese, Afrikaans editions
Christiana Tsai
      Chinese edition
Divine Applications
Heart Cry of China
      Chinese edition
The Holy Spirit and His Work/A.B. Simpson
The Inner Chamber/Andrew Murray
Jewels From The Queen Of The Dark Chamber/Christiana Tsai
      Chinese edition
Key To The Missionary Problem/Andrew Murray
      Nigerian edition
      Portuguese edition
Life—Stop Crowding Me
No Ground
On Your Mark
Powerlines
      Chinese edition
State Of The Church/Andrew Murray

TOUCHING CHINA

"Close Encounters of the Christian Kind"

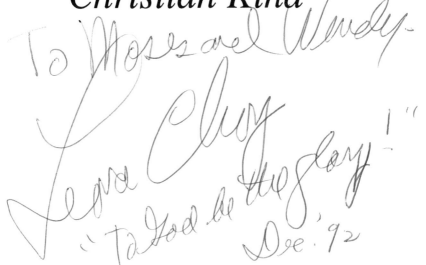

Leona Choy

Unless otherwise indicated, all Scripture references are from the New American Standard Bible, copyright The Lockman Foundation 1960, 1962, 1963, 1968, 1971, 1972, 1973, 1975, 1977. Used by permission.

TOUCHING CHINA: Close Encounters of the Christian Kind
Leona Choy

Copyright © 1992
Published by: Ambassadors For Christ, Inc.
P.O. Box 280, Paradise, PA 17562

Lee Troup: Editorial Advisor
Cover art work and interior sketches by Chinese artists in the People's Republic of China are identified by their Chinese names.
Cover design by Ella Miu

All rights reserved. No part of this publication may be reproduced, stored in a retrieval system, or transmitted, in any form or by any means, electronic, mechanical, photocopying, recording, or otherwise, without the prior written permission of the publisher, except for brief quotations in reviews or articles.

Library of Congress Cataloging-in-Publication Data

Choy, Leona
  Touching China: Close Encounters of the Christian Kind

  Includes bibliographical references.

ISBN 1-882324-00-5
1. Christianity--China. I. Title.

Printed and published in the United States of America

Dedication

I dedicate this book to all the Christians we have met
in China on our journeys to that wonderful land.
And to God's people anywhere in the world
who are privileged to have
"close encounters of the Christian kind"
with the heroic people of China.
Above all, I dedicate this book
to Jesus Christ, Lord of my life.

Acknowledgement

I am grateful to the editorial advice of Lee Troup
of *Ambassadors For Christ, Inc.* and to the constructive
suggestions of other staff members of AFC.
Dr. David Adeney and Dr. Samuel Ling read the manuscript
and offered helpful counsel, as did representatives
of ministries among Chinese students and scholars and
professional service agencies. My husband, Ted, critiqued
many drafts and willingly took over household tasks
while I spent extended time at the computer.

Foreword

When I set sail from England in 1934 with a new group of *China Inland Mission* workers, the age of colonialism was drawing to a close. Soon World War II would shake the very foundations of Western civilization. The great Chinese nation would be torn not only by the invading armies of Japan but also by the civil war that led to the Communist Revolution.

Significant in this period have been the changes of relationship between Western Christians and the Church in China. When we arrived in China in the thirties, we were in a transition period. Some of our senior missionaries remembered Hudson Taylor. They had experienced the life of the early pioneers. The faith, sacrifice, and zeal of our predecessors were a tremendous example to us. However, though young and inexperienced, we were aware of changes taking place.

The Church in China was experiencing the growing pains associated with independence. Following indigenous principles, the *China Inland Mission* was withdrawing its support of pastors and evangelists. Churches were expected to be self-supporting, self-governing, and self-propagating long before the "Three-Self Patriotic Movement."

But the greatest changes took place after our departure from Shanghai in 1950. The Church in China suffered intensely during the years of China's isolation from the rest of the world. What joy to discover on my first return to China in 1978 that not only had God wonderfully preserved and built His Church by the Holy Spirit, but that the Church had experienced phenomenal growth! Despite persecution, restrictions and oppression, the Body of Christ in China is strong and flourishing.

Today we cannot send missionaries to China. But we can encourage Christian students to enroll in Chinese universities to study the language and culture. Christian professionals can serve there in areas of their expertise. We can form meaningful friendships with students and scholars from China in our own communities. God has opened wonderful new doors.

In this book Leona Choy covers these changes and more. She has the great gift of presenting a tremendous amount of information in extremely readable form. She has been in China repeatedly. Her sources are firsthand and her resources are extensive. This book will surely be required reading not only for those who hope to visit or serve in China, but for world Christians trying to understand the multi-faceted situation there today.

I believe that *TOUCHING CHINA* will help us pray with more understanding for the people of that great land and especially for the courageous Chinese Christians.

David H. Adeney
Minister-at-Large
Overseas Missionary Fellowship

Contents

6   Driven Up A Great Wall   45

7   To Market, To Market   56

8   Prosperity Is A "Hot Potato"   65

21 China, Here I Come!   177

22 More About Encounters   189

23 Delivering At The Service Entrance   196

24 Opportunities Around Us   211

1

On The Launching Pad

Who are *you?*

I wrote this book to promote better understanding of China and its people among at least seven categories of readers.

First, for *non-Chinese Christians living in the Western world,* the United States, Canada, Europe, and other non-Asian countries. I hope you will benefit from an overview of the China situation and that your contacts with Chinese friends will be enriched.

Second, may this be a review and update for those of you who are *currently Christian workers among Chinese people* anywhere in the world.

Third, for those of you *seeking God's will for possible ministry among Chinese people* no matter what your age or ethnic background. I hope this book may be a launching pad to help confirm your call.

My fourth and fifth reader categories tend to be similar in outlook: as *Christian Chinese who were born in the West,* you may not have had the advantage of growing up in the mainstream Chinese culture. Perhaps you have been living on the fence between two cultures. You are commonly referred to as ABCs—American-born Chinese. Some of you may be *China-born but a major part of your lives has been spent outside of China.* Some call you ARCs—American-raised Chinese. Your mindset and lifestyle orientation tends to be more Western than Asian. You are basically Chinese but augmented by American influences. Your encounters with people who have been totally raised in China's culture may at times be as unsettling to you as they are to non-Chinese who try to relate to the China-born. Language barriers may exist. Although you are ethnic Chinese, some of you may not be aware of what is happening in the land of your roots, but you are concerned for the welfare of your kinsmen and their spiritual needs.

1

Sixth, it is exciting that God is giving a burden for the evangelism of Chinese people to some of you *Christians from other nations, especially from the Two-thirds world.* Some of your countries have sizeable Chinese communities. As non-Caucasians, you may be uniquely suited for witness in China.

Finally, I hope this book will prove helpful to those of you who are *new Christians, China-born but living temporarily in the West*—students and scholars and your families. You may have little if any knowledge of the history of Christianity in your own country, China's policies toward religion, or information about the growing Christian movement in your homeland. Exploring these topics may help you better understand some things you have experienced.

I have all of you in mind. But to simplify the terminology and sentence structure whenever I refer to my readers, I have directed the text to *non-Chinese Christian.* Those of you who are in the other important categories above please "listen in" for your special transferable concepts. Most of the information should be useful.

Crossing the bridge

Someone said that everything you hear about China is true *somewhere* but not *everywhere.* This may be equally true for our Chinese friends who have come to the West with certain preconceptions.

In this book I have tried to help correct some misinformation and nourish justifiable appreciation and admiration for China and its people. If we are naive or unenlightened about China when we try to cross that "friendship bridge," we may become disillusioned with our close encounters. Or suffer culture shock. I have tried to cushion some of the pothole bumps.

This book is not a how-to-do-it manual. I don't offer detailed instructions to Westerners on how to make friends with students, scholars, and families from China in your communities or how to share your faith with them. But I have provided lists of organizations and agencies that are well-qualified to help. God will lead you in forming those genuine friendships.

I haven't listed specific opportunities in China for Christians to teach and serve. Excellent secular and Christian agencies stand ready to assist you in preparation and job placement. I do share with you reasons

2

for considering such creative approaches and what exciting adventures God may have in store for you.

Because regulations and conditions in China are constantly changing, I have avoided giving logistics of traveling in China—how, when, or where—if you have that wonderful opportunity. Specifics might be out-of-date before this book goes to press. Agencies are available to help you make travel arrangements. My focus is on general useful information, approaches, and attitudes that are likely to remain constant in the foreseeable future. I'll share with you what you might expect on those journeys to China and how to prepare yourself.

Please familiarize yourself with the RESOURCE section in THE BACK OF THE BOOK. Take time *even before you read further* to go over the Glossary of terms, Introduction to the Chinese language, and the Who's Who section. Then you won't be in the dark as we proceed.

The not-so-inscrutable Chinese

What remarkable people the Chinese are! They comprise nearly a quarter of the world's population. Why then do some people refer to Chinese as "inscrutable"?

The dictionary defines "inscrutable" as *incomprehensible, undiscoverable, impenetrable to investigation, not easily understood, mysterious, unfathomable.* If that's what some think, perhaps they have been brainwashed by the fictitious Charlie Chan black-and-white detective movies.

The Chinese aren't a "hidden people." They are found all over the world. It used to be said that the sun never set on the British flag; now it does. But the sun never rises or sets anywhere on this planet without shining on the Chinese.

The Chinese people are "scrutable," which means *capable of being understood by careful study or investigation.* That's what this book is all about. What a complicated and magnificent background our Chinese friends have! I can't tell you *everything you always wanted to know about the Chinese,* but I have tried to provide substantial background to help you feel more confident in your relationships with Chinese people.

But we dare not generalize. Each of the billion-plus Chinese people is as different from one another as are individual Europeans, Africans, Americans, or Indians. At the same time we are all products

3

of our heredity, environment, opportunity—even of our ancient history. Those of us who live in the West can make significant strides in understanding the Chinese through exploring their history and appreciating their struggles.

Why is it important to understand the background of the Chinese people? For a starter, it is vital as a part of world evangelism. We need to know about China's traditional religions, become familiar with her history, and understand the impact of Christianity upon China. And how remarkably God is working in China in the absence of any missionary presence. We need to see the role that Marxist-Leninist politics continue to play in her attitude toward the West today and probably for years to come—no matter what drastic changes *may take place soon.*

A prominent Christian Chinese observer stated, "Our Western Christian interpretation of current China is important. It will affect our approach to China, our attitude, our short-term and long-term program, our relationships with the Chinese, and the way we share the gospel."

No close encounters

For over thirty years the People's Republic of China was largely inaccessible to the average person living in the West. Nearly a billion Chinese people were isolated behind that "bamboo curtain." North Americans seldom had the opportunity to meet anyone who had come from the mainland of China since the 1950s. Few Westerners were able to travel freely in that ancient exotic land, walk on the Great Wall, or visit the Forbidden City and Imperial Palace.

After more than 150 years of faithful pioneer labor in China, Christian missionaries from Western lands had to retreat after the Communist takeover. Only by prayer could the outsider Christian touch the people of China. The Christian world community suffered a great loss both culturally and spiritually by being isolated from *close encounters of the Christian kind* within the People's Republic of China.

Then the picture changed!

Normalization of diplomatic relations between the United States and the People's Republic of China and also between other nations and China transformed the scene. Because of her economic, technological, scientific, and overall world market needs, China opened her door a crack to the West. People exchanges, financial investments, trade, joint business ventures, and other pragmatic contacts escalated. How has this remarkable shift affected our opportunities as Christians for contacts with China's people? Was it good news or bad news?

The good news: We *can* actually touch China today! Her so-called "bamboo curtain" no longer separates her from the outside world. On the other hand, that curtain has not altogether disappeared. The average Westerner may now travel quite freely throughout most of China. China began to permit her students, scholars, and research persons by the thousands to leave China and study in the West. A considerable number of people from the West have been able to serve in China on at least a short-term basis.

However, China officially prohibits missionary work by foreigners. Nevertheless, China is experiencing the greatest explosion of Christian faith among her own people since the gospel was first proclaimed there!

As we explore together the whole panorama of history and happenings in China, we may conclude that none of the above is bad news—*it may all be good news!*

But we want to do more than superficially *touch* China, don't we? We would like *close encounters of the Christian kind* with her people.

So where do we start?

Almost any person in the Americas, Canada, Europe, Australia—nearly anywhere in the world—has the opportunity to MEET Chinese people. I hope this book will help us appreciate that privilege. But how can Christians REACH them to communicate their faith and introduce them to Christ? We need some bridges. Because of the new openness in international relations, we can now have *close encounters with Chinese people* in a number of ways:

(1) *Friendship-witness to transplanted Chinese*: More than forty thousand Chinese students and scholars are currently in the United States! In addition, professors, research persons, privately sponsored

5

immigrants and their families, and individuals who have requested political asylum outside of China have swelled the ranks.

(2) *Using marketable skills to serve in China*: Christians with secular professional credentials may serve in China as teachers, lecturers, researchers, business persons, in government service, etc. Opportunities exist at this writing, though the degree of liberty to share one's faith fluctuates with the political winds.

(3) *Studying in China*: Non-Chinese may enroll in China's institutions to study the Chinese language, culture, or other specialties.

(4) *Tourism to China*: Group tours, special interest tours, and independent travel are all possible, popular, and welcomed by the Chinese government. Because China's leaders are pragmatic, it is highly unlikely that China will ever completely close her door to tourism no matter what happens on the political scene.

(5) *Career missions*: As a traditional vocation usually associated with a mission board or sending agency or religious denomination in a home country this is *not* possible in the People's Republic of China at this writing. But it is possible to serve among the Chinese in many other parts of the world.

What a thrilling opportunity and awesome responsibility God has set before us for *cross-cultural witness* among Chinese people *on whatever turf!* I invite you to fasten your seat belt as we fly first over ancient China and then modern China. May this brief historical survey help us to better understand the Chinese people *in our own communities*—and *in China*. O

2

The *Real* China

China is properly called the PEOPLE'S REPUBLIC OF CHINA or PRC for short. It is inappropriate to call the country Red China or Communist China when we travel there or meet China's people on our turf. Just "China" is fine. Nor should we use "Free China" for Taiwan under the same circumstances.

China got her name from the Ch'in dynasty, one of the shortest (221-207 B.C.). Its fame came in part from the rule of Emperor Shih Huang-ti who unified the language, started the building of the Great Wall, and brought certain reforms.

At this writing, China is still a Communist country following the Marxist-Leninist political philosophy. But she has developed her own modified Communism, referring to herself as a Socialist country. Only about 5 percent (approximately 50 million people) are members of the Communist Party, which came to power in 1949. China has a single party system which is not like a political party in democratic countries to which any citizen can belong.

As we shall explore later, for over a decade the Chinese Communist government has been allowing her people to engage in a considerable measure of private enterprise.

China is *people*

When we think of China, we visualize lots of people. China is understandably worried that her population will exceed the 1.2 billion mark by the year 2000. On April 14, 1989 it already exceeded 1.1 billion. And this despite the "one-child family" policy that the government heavy-handedly enforces throughout China. That means China's population increases at the rate of 1,900 per hour! If the recent birth rate

8

remains unchanged, some 20 million babies will be born every year over the coming decade.

Shanghai, China's largest city and the world's second largest city reached over twelve million by the end of 1988. Its population is expected to escalate with up to 160,000 births in the next five years when a million local women will reach child-bearing age.

Premier Li Peng warned of the urgency of implementing China's existing policy on population limitation by suggesting late marriage, late child-bearing, one-child families, birth control, and abortion. If China loses control of her population increase, the country's modernization drive, ongoing reforms, and efforts to improve the economic environment will be adversely affected, he stated. Water resources are low and grain production is insufficient to sustain population growth. China is nervous.

China has over 600 million young people under 30 years of age. The average age is around 24. China's children number 300 million. China is young!

Most Chinese people, over 90 percent, are of the Han nationality and tend to live in urban areas. Five percent of China's people represent 55 ethnic minorities occupying 60 percent of the land, principally the Western areas, mountains, and deserts. Many have languages of their own.

Some comparisons

China's population is more than 4 times the population of the United States, which is approximately 220 million. China has more people than all of the countries of Africa, Central and South America, and the Caribbean combined.

China's area is nearly 4 million square miles, slightly larger than the U.S. and the third largest country in land area after the former U.S.S.R. and Canada.

China is rich in natural resources and oil, much of which is still untapped.

Her overall climate is similar to the U.S. The Northern climate of Beijing, the capital, is comparable to New England; Guangzhou (Canton) in the South is comparable to Florida.

China has the 6th largest economy in the world and is the world's third largest giver of non-military aid to the Third World.

China's army tops 3.5 million, the second largest standing army in the world, and her air force is the third largest in the world. China has a significant stock of nuclear weapons, ballistic missiles, jet bombers, and radar equipment.

Ninety percent of China's population occupy little more than fifteen percent of the coastal provinces and the central plain. Eighty percent of China's people live in the countryside, but only one-fifth of China's land can be cultivated, resulting in the world's most intensive farming. Wheat in the North and rice in the South are China's predominant crops. Agricultural methods are still quite primitive and China attempts to feed her immense population from her relatively small farming area.

China is behind in industry and much of it is still under central government control. Although the system is being modified somewhat, many urban workers are still assigned to their jobs, provided with housing, education, health services, etc. Some private housing is gradually becoming possible, as well as private education, and other private ownership. The average per capita income of some in on the way up.

Literacy has increased markedly in the past few decades, now around 75 percent, due to compulsory public education, which is still pervaded with a heavy measure of Marxism and Communist-Socialist values.

China has the world's oldest continuous civilization, dating back 4,000 years. For centuries she LOOKED BACKWARD to her Golden Age, her sages, Confucian traditions, classics, and *status quo*. This hindered her early progress as a world power.

After what the Communists called the "Liberation" in 1949, China's dictator, Mao Zedong, tried a GREAT LEAP FORWARD in economy. This attempt in 1958 turned out to be a disastrous LEAP BACKWARD. He had sought to accomplish it in national isolation with poor economic planning, depending largely on forced revolutionary motivation.

After Mao's death in 1976, Vice Premier Deng Xiaoping's pragmatic reform program launched a GREAT LEAP OUTWARD toward a 20 year modernization program. For the first time, China began to invite the cooperation and expertise of Western nations.

The largest scale social and economic revolution in China's history took place over the last half-century with politics dominating all of life for the Chinese people in an unprecedented way. Some notable achievements were made through complete totalitarian control, but at the sacrifice of the lives of millions of Chinese people and the loss of personal liberties.

The sweep of history

The Chinese had sages when Europeans were still savages! Let's have a capsulized history lesson of this advanced civilization. From about 2000 B.C. to A.D. 1911 China was ruled by a succession of dynasties and control was vested in emperors. Rulers were regarded as holding their authority by the "mandate of heaven" with the moral order of the state committed to them. From ancient days China put great value on the search for harmony in architecture, nature, politics, human relationships, and the mind. Even her writing seeks for harmony, balance, and beauty. The famous Ming dynasty about which tourists hear so much lasted from A.D. 1368 to 1644, under which Beijing (Peking) was rebuilt and a distinctive architecture and culture blossomed.

A feudal society existed for most of those centuries with the elite class exploiting the peasants to finance its own lavish and indulgent life style. From the mid-1600s to 1911 the Manchus, the Ch'ing dynasty, governed China. During that period culture flourished even more, but trouble and instability were rocking the government. The culprits were the ever-present Westerners who threatened domination of China's trade and pushed their colonial and imperial interests.

A very fragile Chinese Republic was formed in 1911 under Dr. Sun Yat-sen, but difficulties continued to loom large and warlords disrupted government. Natural disasters devastated the people and repeated calamities made the nation ripe for revolution.

General Chiang Kai-shek vied for leadership with his Kuomintang Nationalist Party while the Chinese Communist Party, which had been formed in 1921, began to challenge it. The two parties cooperated briefly against the military might of Japan which in 1938 had threatened to overrun China. Eventually they turned on one another in a full-scale civil war.

After inflicting incredible devastation on China and its people, the Japanese surrendered in 1945. With the defeat of the Nationalists, the Communists proclaimed their "liberation" of China on October 1,

11

1949 by taking complete control of the country. Chiang moved with his Nationalist government to the island of Taiwan, maintaining that his government alone represented the Chinese people.

The Communists, with a Chinese version of Marxist-Leninism, have ruled China to the present. Communism claimed to attack the pressing problems of the peasants and the workers, their poverty, exploitation by the landlord class, and foreign interference in national affairs. Party Chairman Mao Zedong was called the "Great Helmsman" but instead of alleviating the problems of his people, he steered China's ship of state into an even worse period of suffering. Through the ten year "Great Proletarian Cultural Revolution" instigated by Mao, it attacked the old Confucian system with its social elitism and traditional values. Youthful radicals were turned loose to destroy "old ideologies, old customs, old morals, and old habits." They took over and demolished government buildings, schools, churches and temples, beat and publicly humiliated officials, administrators, teachers, and religious leaders. That period was rightly called a blood bath.

After Mao's death in 1976, a more reformist, pragmatic regime came into power led by Deng Xiaoping. It began to distance itself from the radical revolutionary line, and was characterized by a drive toward socialist modernization and a more open attitude toward the outside world.

China's religious pillars

China developed a unique synthesis of her three religions of past centuries, which did not require the exclusive allegiance of its adherents to any one of them. It would be more accurate to refer to two religions and one system of ethics because Confucianism is not considered a religion.

CONFUCIUS, born in the Chou dynasty in 551 B.C., was China's best known moral philosopher. He was not a religious teacher because he did not speak of a supernatural being. He referred only to a moral force in the universe. His ideas formed the moral code of China's upper classes right into the twentieth century. His concepts were feudal in that their established ceremonies recognized outright class distinctions. His teaching centered around the family and its harmony as the hub of society, the state as its extension, and all other relationships functioning in a *status quo* order. Confucianism chained the Chinese people for centuries forcing them to accept their unchangeable lot in life. Confucius was never worshipped as a deity or a prophet but his teachings and writings shaped China's social and political structure.

TAOISM is a mystical philosophy/religion, a reaction against the hard realities of this world. It is native and has a history of more than 1,700 years. As a religion it is polytheistic and linked with folk religion. It opposed war, the struggle for power, status, and wealth. It was a thinker's philosophy. The individual was considered important only as a part of the whole great pattern of nature, called Tao, literally "The Way," in a metaphysical sense. Founded by Lao-Tzu, whom some say may have been a myth himself, it is a passive philosophy based on lack of desire as being the ideal state. Its doctrines are based on the writings, the *Tao-te Ching*.

BUDDHISM is China's largest religion today with officially over 80 million followers. It is also an escape religion, originating in Central Asia some 2,000 years ago and spreading in many directions. Readily accepted by the Chinese, it perceives "reality" as illusory, including the idea of self. It taught that if a person becomes "enlightened" and comes to realize that self is only an illusion that leads to misery and suffering in this world, he is extinguished at death like a candle flame going out. At that point he is said to enter Nirvana, which is non-existence, thought to be the coveted final state. If a person is not "enlightened," he must be reborn (reincarnated) and his life-flame is transferred to a new candle and continues the illusion of existing. Buddhism held a strong appeal for Chinese since the adherent could still hold on to certain aspects of Confucianism and Taoism and folk beliefs. Of all the religious communities in China, the Buddhist is said to be the largest.

Add to the mixture...

ANCESTOR WORSHIP pre-dated the above religions and was often incorporated into all three. Since ancestors were thought to still be alive and influencing the affairs of men for good or evil, they had to be placated with offerings of food and incense and worshipped. It is condemned by the Chinese government as a superstition.

ISLAM, another foreign religion, filtered into China with the barbarians from the North and West more than 1,300 years ago. Islam, or the Muslim religion, is on the rise in modern China with about 15

13

million adherents mostly among the minority nationalities.

We can see how CHRISTIANITY, approaching China as still another "foreign religion," tended to be resisted. It had a significant difference, however, because it insisted on a "One Way" conversion with exclusive allegiance and no syncretism. It clashed with the easygoing Chinese tradition of religious compromise whereby the individual simply added anything beneficial to his worship roster. O

3

Chronic Xenophobia

Because China considers herself exploited, manipulated, and abused by foreigners in the past, she has developed chronic "xenophobia." Though not a disease, it is transmitted from generation to generation and is contagious. Xenophobia is defined as *an unreasonable fear or hatred of foreigners and strangers or of that which is foreign or strange.*

China had nothing but trouble with foreigners since the first ones came to take a greedy look at her assets centuries ago. In China's view, pushy foreigners caused all her problems. They forced China to buy opium against her will, demanded diplomatic immunity, preferential treatment, and—brought along their missionaries to force "foreign religion" down the throats of what was the most civilized nation in the world at that time. At least that's what it looked like to the Chinese. Was the picture accurate? Judge for yourself after we add a few details of history.

The British pushed aside the morally questionable nature of their opium traffic because they were blinded by the enormous financial profits from pushing "chemical happiness." When the West didn't find a "Welcome Mat" for trade at the front door of China, foreigners attempted to pry open the reluctant mouth of dragon China by force-feeding opium. They hoped that would speed her decay and weaken her defenses.

China was resolute. As a matter of historical record, she did not want opium or any drugs, and did everything in her power to resist them. An imperial decree in China forbade the use of opium except for medicinal purposes. She officially pleaded with Britain to stop its import. China's cause fell on deaf ears and the Opium War of 1839-1842 was fought over the matter. The Chinese were easily defeated by Western military firepower and were no match against trained and experienced manpower. What irony that some of the same countries that pushed drugs on China are now experiencing the most devastating drug problem in history!

The victorious foreigners imposed a long series of indignities upon China. The infamous Treaty of Nanking humiliated the Chinese into signing away the island of Hong Kong to Britain for a hundred years. Time is up in 1997! Moreover, the barbarian foreigners then forced China to open her doors to trade and to allow foreigners to live in five Chinese ports without being subject to China's laws. China had to pay millions of dollars to Britain in reparations for damages during the wars. Not a pretty picture?

Hitchhiking imperialism

There's more. Not only Britain but America and other Western nations should assume some blame. They traded in opium as well and eased into China on the privileges gained by Britain through the Unequal Treaties. One historian described America's role as "hitchhiking imperialism" since America reaped all the financial and commercial advantages gained by other nations through force.

Eventually foreigners controlled most of China's overseas trade. In 1853 the British, Americans, and French took over Chinese port customs. Another war followed, another Chinese defeat, and under the Tientsin Treaties both the opium trade and missionary activities were legalized—strange bedfellows. Foreigners even exported Chinese to their colonial territories as cheap labor. Germany and Russia joined in the wars and licked their economic lips as they enjoyed the spoils. Western nations didn't give up The Unequal Treaties until World War II despite China's repeated pleas for their abolition.

Do we feel uncomfortable? Ashamed? Shocked by indisputable historical realities? Can we now understand China's xenophobia? Wouldn't a nation that had been forced to bow her neck for so long be proud of the fact that she was finally strong and independent enough to declare, "We have stood up!"?

Other related factors in China's background will also help us understand present day China and our friends who have come from that land.

An ego-centric view

In China's capital city, the ancient Temple of Heaven built in 1420 is topped with a round stone. It supposedly marks the center of the earth as determined by Chinese geographers and sages thousands of years ago. It is a meaningful symbol of the ancient Chinese way of thinking that *China was the center of the world.* The Chinese characters that make up the word *China* are *Zhongguo*, which means "Middle Kingdom." The Chinese were convinced that everything revolved around China.

For more than 4,000 years the rulers and people were absolutely convinced of China's superiority. They fully expected all barbarians (everyone else in the world outside of China's borders) to look up to China. Literally to kneel and prostrate themselves. When they did not do so, the Chinese thought, *How dare those Western invaders enter the presence of the Chinese Emperor, the Son of Heaven, as if they were equals!* When merchants arrived on China's shores from the West, they were *not* welcomed with open arms. They had taken for granted that China would like to trade with the rich West and acquire its fancy commodities. China surprised and dismayed them, snubbing early tradesmen. Why should she want anything from barbarians? She maintained that she already had everything she needed.

Westerners, on their part, *considered themselves superior* to the people in this "heathen" land. The Chinese, on the other hand, looked down upon the big-nosed, red-bearded savages. Both assumed a fencing stance and military and cultural clashes were inevitable.

Gross humiliation

Most countries have their national superiority complexes but perhaps not to the extent that China has. She felt justified because of her ancient, remarkably advanced civilization. We can see what a shock and humiliation it was for China when foreigners forced her at gunpoint to accept foreign enclaves. Like parasites on a host plant or animal they attached themselves to her and hung on! Incredibly, those invaders maintained that they even had immunity from China's laws. Within their self-determined boundaries the barbarians insisted on doing their own thing.

Reverse that and imagine our reaction if invaders from China or any other nation attempted something similar on our turf.

Isolationist defense

No wonder China built a literal Great Wall in an attempt to protect herself against the barbarian world. And in more recent years, pulled down her bamboo curtain and isolated herself for several decades. China was shocked when Japan like a feisty little terrier compared to monstrous dragon China had the nerve to come over and fight on China's soil, overrun her militarily, rape and massacre her people, and attempt to conquer her.

Inevitably, China realized that the world was shrinking. She could no longer keep her doors shut against it. Others nations were thrusting themselves upon her economically and her sheltered society would never be the same again.

In international political ideologies and conflicts China became forced to take sides in order to survive. She chose a side, the Communist one, and contended that she needed time to work out her gargantuan internal problems in isolation. She didn't want any help—or hindrance—from the outside world. She ushered out or forced out all foreigners and everything they represented, including religion, and those trouble-making missionaries (in her view). China wanted time to contextualize the political ideology she had espoused (although Communism, too, was a foreign political ideology). That continued to be China's rationale for national isolation during the next thirty-some years after she had proudly declared that she "stood up."

The bloody fist

To carry out that plan, the radical Communist revolutionary, Chairman Mao Zedong, strode boldly on stage. He was the architect of that bloody and blasphemous era that was called the "Cultural Revolution" (1966-1976). Today's China, in retrospect, labels it as the greatest catastrophe in her history. It was blasphemous because the government required her citizens to revere Chairman Mao as more than a man, almost an infallible deity. His words and writings were pawned off on

19

China's people as sacred, to be slavishly obeyed. The religious cult of leader-worship was politically motivated. It was a means to whip China's masses into a cohesive, manageable shape in the shortest possible time.

How could the leadership maintain control of such scattered masses? Obviously, by eliminating all counter-revolutionaries. Not only foreigners, with whom she had already dealt, but any of China's own people whose thoughts had previously been tainted by them. Intellectuals, scholars, landowners, the wealthy, the religious, regardless of which religion, the bourgeois class—all had to be erased from Mao's new dream-picture of China. The blood of China's people literally ran down the streets of her cities and countryside and soaked into the Good Earth of China.

Her internal revolution eventually failed miserably, and her thirty-plus years of insulated, isolated struggle left her debilitated. But with remarkable and predictable resilience, China emerged, licking her wounds, declaring proudly, "We're *still* standing!" She is letting the outside world know, in no uncertain terms, that she is in control of her own destiny and she will continue to stand ramrod erect.

Deep roots

China's memory is longer than an elephant's. China determined never again to let herself be forced into a position of accepting foreign influence and control. Every nation would have to deal eye-to-eye with her from now on. That resolution seems to be behind all her dealings with internal and international matters. Her perpetual grudge and apprehension toward foreigners may seem exaggerated and needless to us, but doubtless it is perfectly consistent to the Chinese mind and culture.

Let's remember, however, that China's political position as a Communist country doesn't overshadow the fact that she is an ancient civilization. Her way of life is steeped in thousands of years of "Chineseness." Her outlook remains more Chinese than Communist/socialist—a recent garment she has put on that hasn't been fitting too well. Her ancient heritage continues to affect her present bearing. She still views the world through Chinese eyes. Political ideologies may come and go in China, but her roots will remain deep in her own Chinese soil.

Who's afraid of the big bad wolf?

Houses and apartments in China, Hong Kong, and many countries traditionally have layers of doors at the same entrance. The outer one may have strong bars like a cage or prison. And each door has its own key. When we borrowed the apartment of friends in Hong Kong, they gave us a ring of keys, all different, to open the layers of doors.

It should come as no surprise that China is presently still cautious and suspicious toward outsiders. She has only opened her outer door a crack and is keeping a barred inner door in place against potential invasions—whether ideological, material, political, or religious. China has more than one door and one key if outsiders would gain entrance today. But she insists on holding tight to the key ring herself.

A Central Committee Communist Party member declared at a public gathering, "Let not people think that because we have opened our door in some measure that we do not distinguish between wolves and friends." Remember the children's story about the big bad wolf who used many tricks to try to get into the house of the three little pigs? Or the wolf who disguised himself as the gentle grandmother of Little Red Riding Hood in order to eat her up?

China also has her fables and legends about wolves. She is suspicious of any who disguise their features and voices and purposes while intending to "eat her up" again.

There are more parallels to the China situation in the story of the "Three Little Pigs." The big bad wolf threatened that he would "huff and puff and blow their house down." They knew they were safe as long as they stayed securely inside. So the wolf tried to maneuver them to come out. He lured them with various appointments to meet him, but they outsmarted him each time. Finally they tricked the wolf into coming down their chimney into a boiling pot—and that was the end of the wolf. The little pigs had wolf stew for dinner.

Let's give the story a little twist and try a different ending. Presently, China has at least partially opened her door to the "big bad wolves" of the West, whom for centuries she considered barbarians. Thank God the West didn't attempt a *military* invasion to get in, or else well-meaning foreign missionaries might have arrived on gunboats (or military transport planes) again. The West waited, perhaps impatiently, until China was hungry for Western technology and the other necessities for her modernization program to catch up with the rest of the world.

The Western wolf said, "I'll meet you at the marketplace." China fell for the lure—or the West did, depending on which side really initiated the invitation. At least East has met West at the world market to deal with one another.

Have the three little pigs (the people of China) been eaten up by the big bad wolf of Western capitalism after all? And has that which they feared come upon them? When the door was first ajar, much rhetoric came out of China's press warning against "the decadent West." China insisted that she wanted only "the good" (in her definition) and not "the bad" (in her definition). But the flies, mosquitoes, and vermin of the West managed to slip in with the good that China welcomed. Drugs, disco, pornography, prostitution, loose living, greed for money, corruption, have proliferated in China. Not all were brought in from the West, of course. The stage was already set for the unleashing of the corruption that was already in the hearts of unregenerate people in China. It is the same corruption that is in the hearts of unregenerate people in the West or anywhere else.

The "Wicked Witch" of the West

The *South China Morning Post*, November 1988, observed,

[Shanghai and China as a whole]. . . are taking up the West's wicked ways. Vice was outlawed by Mao Zedong's Communist revolution in the 1950s, mobsters were slung out, opium dens were smashed, prostitutes became factory workers, bars were shut down, and venereal disease was nearly eradicated. . . . But 12 years after Mao's death Shanghai is sliding back into some of its old ways, spearheading what conservatives fear is a wave of decadence brought about by China's decade-old policy of opening up to the outside world. . . . A moral laxity threatens a society barely a decade out of its prudish Maoist conformity and only 40 years from strict Confucian etiquette. *Growing prosperity may not be worth the contamination. . . .*

But a leading sociologist from Shanghai's Academy of Social Sciences, Mr. Su Songxing, looked at it from a different perspective. He perceived that China faces a much deeper problem than the open door policy—and it should not all be laid at the feet of Western or foreign contamination again. He maintained that the Cultural Revolution destroyed China's traditional values and at the same time weakened its Communist ideology. But, he said, *it put nothing in their place.*

As Christians, we know that a condition of emptiness and hopelessness is the ultimate despair for an individual or a nation. A house swept clean of the negative *but not replaced with something positive* will be worse in the end.

Squeaky clean and puritanical?

Could we in the West have been so gullible as to fall for the propaganda that came out of Communist China especially in the '60s and '70s? We read incredible statements in our secular press, the liberal Christian press, and even sometimes in the evangelical press on what a pure, morally purged, and clean society Chairman Mao had succeeded in creating. No vice and crime, everyone smiling and filled with altruistic idealism, politically correct, patriotically and selflessly "serving the people," no one seeking his own, but all working for the common good. We were supposed to believe that utopia or the millennium had arrived. China was said to have achieved this idyllic state without God and religious morality. We were told that Communism succeeded where the missionaries had failed. Many in the West were naively advocating, "We should all learn from China."

Even evangelical Christian writings sometimes reflected a distorted picture:

> One must search hard in the cities of new China for the decadence, squalor, and raw sin that once gave pungency to the word 'Shanghai.' A high sense of common purpose, puritanical labor, and public morality is widely reported by those who are moving through the new windows into China. . . .The new ethics of China are similar to those of early Christianity. . . .

23

I will refrain from listing the source above. We found out later that the new, supposedly moral ethics of China was just a veneer, a slick propaganda ploy. The government was forcibly suppressing crime, immorality, and unlawful conduct by heavy-handed means. The government meted out capital punishment when it discovered transgressions. Ironically, this was the same government which had murdered its own people by the millions!

Morality had been legislated in China. It didn't come from within the individual. It was a false, temporary morality, from which the lid has now been removed by allowing certain liberties. The normal festering corruption of humanity without God is spilling out with all its stench. Communism failed and will always fail to "create the new man." Capitalism or democracy or any other human framework, will also fail to regenerate man and make him morally pure. ○

4

Building On An Earthquake Fault

C hina has been building a nation that appears to have a revolving glass door above an earthquake fault. Her government is like a disaster waiting to happen. Let's take a sweeping aerial view of the historical landscape. After this summary, in the chapters that follow, we'll land and take a closer look at different aspects of China's society.

Throughout her long history, access from the outside has been through a revolving door. Foreigners are never sure whether they are going *in* or are on their way *out*. We have seen that China always felt threatened by "barbarians"—anyone not Chinese. She had never put out a permanent "welcome mat" to foreigners whom she viewed as exploiters—which they usually were. China had suffered too many times at the hands of greedy nations who often took advantage of her resources and consumer potential.

During the early years of Communist rule and the internal political ferment that came with it, Mao's hard line dictatorship ruled every aspect of people's lives and work. Thought control repressed any independent ideas or attempts to realize personal freedoms. China totally closed her door to outside influence during the "Cultural Revolution."

She dramatically opened it again in the late 1970s. After Mao's death and the leadership power struggle that followed, a more moderate regime took control under Vice Premier Deng Xiaoping—a reformer but still firmly in the Communist camp. A softer line prevailed, at least on the surface. The door started to revolve again and the outside world rushed in for business, curiosity, and cultural exchanges, all the while eyeing China as a massive consumer market.

China's leaders seemed to be taking a strange direction for a totalitarian Marxist state. Private enterprise was suddenly encouraged, personal profit-making was permitted, education was "in" again, foreign investment was wooed, foreign experts and corporate capitalists were welcomed to establish joint ventures. A 1.25 billion dollar annual tourism industry mushroomed and friendly foreigners were climbing the Great Wall and drinking cokes in the Forbidden City.

The revolving door also permitted China's students and scholars to study overseas to acquire the scientific and technological expertise China needed to catch up with the rest of the world. Not a completely impossible dream given her massive work force and population.

But in early summer 1989 the world gasped as mass student, worker, and people demonstrations for freedom were followed by a bloody massacre at Tiananmen Square. That was followed by a military crackdown on all protesters, dissidents, and "counter-revolutionaries." History repeated itself as the revolving door spilled out fearful Westerners retreating until the muddy waters cleared.

A fresh breeze blowing?

China's economic reforms had been gathering speed for a decade—but political reforms did not keep pace. Hard line Marxist Party leaders, mostly aged men, opposed most of Deng's reforms dubbing them capitalistic and bourgeois. From time to time China felt earthquake tremors when the hard liners attempted to overthrow the reformers and return China to the iron grip of orthodox Marxists.

The rumbling and shaking of another earthquake accelerated when China finally opened to the West and sent her scholars there. Freedom ideas blew into China like fresh breezes. Students and scholars returning from the West began to taste democracy and relish individual liberties. Tourists, businessmen, and teachers from the West were also carriers of new ideas.

Students in China's own universities could now read books and literature that were formerly forbidden, and this exposure fanned the fires of desire for more freedom. Radio broadcasts from overseas were no longer on the forbidden list. The Voice of America enlightened the people in a way their own censored media did not. Television, American movies and videos, all contributed to the growing restlessness of

27

China's urban and educated population.

The people realized that what their Communist leaders called "liberation" was only another form of imprisonment. By fostering material reforms and allowing the people to experience a somewhat higher standard of living and acquire certain luxury items, the Communist rulers were resorting to powerful sedatives, so to speak, to keep citizens docile under a continuing Marxist regime. Freedom of the press and speech, the privilege of making one's own choices, of trying to change what the majority feels should be changed—these were still denied.

Mixed reactions

The older generation with history in perspective is generally allowing its fires for radical change to burn low. But the younger generation that did not go through the devastating "Cultural Revolution" or taste blood for its convictions, is burning for genuine change. With courage and guts youths are risking their lives in a jail break for freedoms we take for granted in the West.

Unfortunately, not only fresh, healthy ideas came into China with the opening doors to the Western world. Many Chinese teens and young adults embraced some of the wilder, more reckless aspects of the American youth culture. They have adopted radical dress styles, music, and values, tossing aside moral restraints in a slavish imitation of American movies, videos, and records. Of course exposure to another culture can't be totally blamed for increased degradation. But in China the youth are receiving a rocket boost in immorality from trying to be like the Americans they see depicted in the media.

We'll examine most of the above trends in more detail in the chapters that follow. Next we'll take a closer look at those decadent rumblings that began shaking China in the decade or so just before the Tiananmen Square demonstrations. O

28

5

Down The Moral
Roller Coaster

The delirious pursuit of materialism has put the United States, as well as other countries, on a roller coaster speeding down the rails *morally*. We removed the teaching of moral absolutes from our educational system and legislated religion out of the classrooms. A generation or two has grown up without inner restraints, indulging themselves as if there were no tomorrow. A recital of the escalating deadly ills of *our own society*, of whose stench we are acutely aware, is superfluous. Unchecked, the result will be as terminal for any modern civilization as it was for Rome when it crumbled.

Is there any evidence that China may be heading down that same course?

The "Boss Man" speaks

"China's greatest mistake over the past 10 years has been insufficient attention to *moral education*" declared none other than senior Chinese leader Deng Xiaoping in March 1989. In Chinese Communist terminology, the words "moral" and "spiritual" are not used in a theological sense. Morality by Communist standards is perceived as orderly conduct, good behavior, and politically correct attitudes.

Deng admitted that in the process of economic development and the attempt to raise people's living standards, the State gave inadequate instructions to Communist Party members and citizens to adhere to the traditions of hard work and plain living. "After careful and sober-minded consideration, we have come to the conclusion that this spiritual problem is more important than inflation," Deng said. Other official Chinese journals echoed his complaint about the lack of moral standards and ethics among the people at large. They were alarmed that it had expressed itself in "festering corruption *at every level—top to bottom.*" Let's briefly review what China's own media had to say about its nationwide decline of morals and ethics in the months *just prior* to the 1989 Tiananmen massacre. Did the students demonstrating for democracy and "against corruption" have their facts straight?

Bureaucratic profiteering

An alarming increase in major graft and bribery cases began to appear on China's court dockets. Some young people in charge of money and materials had been embezzling public funds and committing other economic crimes, according to *Jingji Ribao* (Economic Daily). Criminal partnerships emerged. The number of leading cadre, unit leaders, all the way to high government officials who engaged in economic crimes was rising. Many embezzlers juggled accounts for profit, even committing their crimes with the aid of sophisticated computers.

Newspapers reported that a large number of offenders spent their illicit gains on expensive commodities, fancy eating, drinking, and gambling. How similar is the expression of human nature whether in the East or West!

The *Gongren Ribao* (Workers' Daily) reported that prestigious government retirees took advantage of their positions and influence by obtaining goods in great demand and then reselling them at higher prices, cheating both state and people. The newspaper called this practice "a pollution to the social environment of China" and pointed an accusing finger at dishonest officials who backed such offenders and allowed them to flourish.

Apparently too close a link existed between the government and enterprises, making racketeering easy. According to this report,

> Many retirees still hold influence. They make connections to get precious goods by discreet notes and phone calls. On the other end of the scale, relying on their parents' prestige, the children of high-ranking officials

31

can also obtain luxury items and none dares cross them.

Companies set up for unreasonable profit sprang up every-where, and prices of high-demand commodities soared.

Power worship

Another Chinese newspaper pointed at the abuse of power all through the ranks of government and society. Status and position of any kind brings whatever degree of power comes with that rank. Overlording by public officials, tax collectors, policemen, teachers, and customs officers was common. The newspaper *Lilun Xinxi Bao* noted,

> In our society some people regard power as more valuable than money. They try their best to transform power into property. . . by the unhealthy tendency to take bribes, accept dinners, and receive gifts. . . . Writing a slip of paper is power; a ticket is power; and a signature is power.

Welcome to the club. In the West such things are familiar to us from grass roots to high government.
An article in an April 1989 issue of *Guangming Daily* declared,

> Politics goes hand in hand with morality. Embezzlement, bribery, dirty tricks to make money, undercutting others, and generally breaking the law—all indicate a moral deterioration in China today. Traditionally, the relation-ship between the ruler and the subjects constituted the core of Chinese ethics. Political obedience by the subjects was of paramount ethical importance. . . . Chinese politics was seemingly morals-oriented. . . . This actually turned political compulsion into moral compulsion, which was reinforced by clanship ethics. . . . When the ruler was politically strong, morality had a powerful, binding influ-ence on society. But once political power degenerated, ethical bonds were broken, and corruption became wide-spread. Political and moral decadence set off each other. . . .

The article concluded that morality-oriented politics and politics-oriented morality had been strong during the founding of the PRC but the "Cultural Revolution" abused it by imposing the social ethics it desired. Unfortunately, the past decade of reforms loosened morality and substituted modernization as the focus of national consciousness. Social productivity was the yardstick; evils proliferated.

Solutions bound to fail

What solution does China offer? The above article suggested,

The average Chinese, having experienced yo-yo changes in his or her ethical notions and values, will never again relapse into the old ethics of blind, sheep-like obedience. *An alternative ethical system that would provide social restraints has yet to emerge.* Restraints on morality are weakening. . . .Nothing has taken their place to keep people's behavior from overstepping the limits of propriety.

This is a perceptive analysis. But it stopped short of the theological solution—the only one that would give people the power to be moral. The article continued,

The solution lies in re-establishing human relationships on principles of justice and fairness. This can only be achieved by intensifying reform. A code of professional ethics for government officials and civil servants should be enforced by political and economic institutions to eliminate sources of corruption. Cultivation of the people's sense of self-restraint should also be strengthened.

From a Christian world view we know that the solutions proposed are idealistic, unrealistic dreams without the inner changes that are only possible by spiritual re-birth through Christ. Codes of ethics and self-restraint and unending reforms have never been able to legislate morality in human beings in any culture throughout history.

33

Invasion of toy soldiers

Consider China's children. To its credit, China thought about banning the showing of the Chinese version of "The Transformers," an American television cartoon, because it was too violent and would exert a harmful influence on China's children. Chinese legislators said that the cartoon depicted "bellicose robot characters with limitless supernatural powers who would poison the minds of young children." But the cartoon created a huge demand for imported "Transformer" toys that were excessively expensive. A set cost about 1,000 yuan, nearly one year's income for an average worker in China!

Just before Spring Festival 1989, one toy shop in Beijing sold 800,000 yuan worth of "Transformer" toys in two months and another department store reported 300,000 yuan in sales in two weeks. "Nearly 90 percent of Beijing's children have one," boasted the happy spokesman for the Beijing Department Store as it applauded the profits.

After the toys lost popularity in the U.S. market in 1986, shrewd American merchandisers set their sights on China as a potential massive consumer market for them—which it proved to be. Millions of Chinese viewers became obsessed with the television series and "fascinated children were crazed and lured into toy shops in droves."

Commenting on recent toy fads in China, a citizen declared in *Beijing Review*, March 1989,

> This is an indirect result of the country's family planning policy, which has produced more and more one-child families. Many parents regard children as the major source of their own happiness. Young parents who are now better paid than their own parents, usually look for toys to please their children. On the principle of anything for the children, particularly if they think the toy is educational, Chinese parents are paying out between 400 and 700 yuan at a time to feed the growing craze for video games.

China Daily, April 1989, reported that during the first two months of that year, sets that connect into television for display are moving to the top as best seller toys to the value of over 1 million yuan. Introduced to China only since 1985, video games grew in popularity

34

as living standards rose.

Honesty the best policy?

Not all who have "become well off first," as the Chinese express it, are honest and benevolent. The Chinese press carried on a heated debate of opinions among ordinary people about whether free enterprise is suitable for China today. According to *Liao Wang* (Outlook Weekly), some people said,

> In the present circumstances, many have grown rich by stealing, grafting, taking more than their share or travelling around selling goods for more than they are worth. We law-abiding people cannot become rich. Encouraging those with indecent motives to "become well off first" means cutting our flesh to feed them.

On the other side, comments were,

> Rich is better than poor. Everyone can benefit from the country's prosperity. Units and people who become well off first can carry others to prosperity along with them. Industry naturally develops from small to large; business develops from poor to good; and a country develops from a closed to an open-door policy. . . .It is a good thing for the poor to become prosperous. But it is bad that some people have become rich through dishonest means. All statements must be based on this point. Unhealthy tendencies must not be encouraged.

Apparently some judges in China don't have clean hands either. Judicial and court officials and bailiffs have been disciplined and punished for breaches of discipline or law. The cases involved lack of honesty in handing down judgments, benefiting from lavish banquets given in their honor, the receiving of valuable gifts, bribes, extortion, gambling privileges, and fringe benefit visits to prostitutes, according to the *Xinhua* newspaper, May 1989.

35

Tax evasion—China style

Cheating on taxes knows no geographic boundaries. More than 80 percent of Shanghai's 110,000 private businessmen have evaded taxes to some extent, officials say. In April 1989 the *China Daily* reported,

> Tax evasion undermines society. A Chinese pop singer evaded taxes of more than 30,000 yuan from ticket receipts. It's deplorable that more and more people who earn high incomes are evading taxes. . . not only the self-employed, but it is an open secret that more and more white-collar workers are following suit. Many have taken advantage of loopholes in the reform to get rich. Hence a nationwide moral degradation. . . . .Even if modernization were achieved, one would feel extremely sad to live among the morally degenerate.

Begging with a new flair

In October 1989 *Beijing Review* stated that although China never completely eliminated begging, a new kind of beggar has recently appeared who makes an easy living in a "new profession."

A recent investigation showed that only 20 percent of beggars seen in public places are doing so from true hardship. The rest are able-bodied men and women who act pitifully to take advantage of the public. In some places a beggar is able to make more than 100 yuan a day, the equivalent of an ordinary worker's earnings for a whole month. One man from Anhui Province built new houses for his three sons with the money he earned from begging. Children and teenagers make up 25 percent of beggars and steal in addition to begging. With their easy profits they eat, drink, watch violent videotapes and go to dance halls. Some beg in the day and prostitute or gamble at night.

Would you believe—the lottery?

Gambling, an age-old vice in China, is making a comeback after being officially banned following the birth of new China in 1949. In one year in Beijing alone police arrests for gambling exceeded 10,000. Gamblers come from all walks: farmers, government employees, the self-employed, unemployed youngsters, university and middle school students, Communist Party members and leaders, and teachers. They include young and old. In May 1989 *China Daily* reported,

> Gambling stakes are becoming bigger and bigger. Professional gamblers play for keeps. The competition among rivals often results in bloody fights and gives rise to crime. For gamblers, the lure is the possibility of winning big; but once hooked, there is no way out. Addiction and obsession take over. Thousands of women in Changsha, capital of Hunan Province, have joined police in the fight against gambling.

The *China Women's News* ran the story that women, by working together, last year closed 475 gambling dens resulting in the arrest of 3,600 gamblers.

Mahjongg, a game of Chinese origin played with domino-like tiles, was banned during the revolution. In recent years it spread like wildfire again throughout China. In one township in suburban Nanhui County with a population of about 10,000, there are 7,000 mahjongg players, many gambling for high stakes.

Holding a lottery ticket of any kind was once regarded as a form of gambling, and the practice was officially banned in 1987. Now it is once again thriving throughout China—and this time it is sponsored by the bank, reported *China Daily*, May 1989. In a savings deposit lottery, the bank sells 20,000 tickets for 30 yuan each and the top prize is a refrigerator worth 2,500 yuan. The smallest winner gets a bar of toilet soap and a towel!

But everyone who buys a ticket wins, in one sense. Supposedly each will get back his capital, the ticket price but without interest, in two years. The lottery was an inducement to people to put their considerable spare cash into savings deposits instead of buying expensive consumer goods. But it was viewed by some officials as "stimulating people's

37

psychology for speculation and encouraging gambling."

A rerun of social diseases

In the Shanghai area alone, venereal disease sufferers increased four to five times during the first quarter of 1989. Most were under 30. The alarming annual average increase since 1984 has been 3.7 times. In the mid-1988s the *Beijing Review* assessed the situation:

> After the founding of the PRC, it took China 15 years to eradicate VD. But less than 20 years later, such diseases, almost forgotten by all, began quietly to re-occur. People from abroad are obviously the initial source of infection—not only foreigners, but people from Hong Kong and Macao. The re-spread of prostitution, tendencies toward sexual freedom, lack of basic morality, and "sex gangs" are contributing factors. More than 70 percent of the patients are male, and the diseases are especially prevalent among criminal gangs, prostitutes, and purchasing agents and salesmen who have relatively high incomes and often travel alone around the country.

AIDS too? *Beijing Review* in January 1989 reported, "China fights back threat of AIDS" The *South China Morning Post*, December 1988, stated,

> A health official in Beijing has warned that it will be impossible to stop the spread of AIDS in China because of the country's open door policy and steady increases of premarital sex and prostitution. . . .The only measures we can take now [are aimed at trying] to limit its spread.

China banned the import of blood products in 1984 in an effort to halt AIDS transmission. Public health sources said that both homosexual and promiscuous heterosexual contacts, and especially premarital sex by China's youth were major means of contamination. China requires all foreigners who plan to reside in China—except diplomats—to take an AIDS test. But AIDS is still alarmingly escalating in China.

Drugs—back where we started

According to *Beijing Review*, February 1989, there were about 20 million drug addicts in China in 1949. Only three years after the founding of New China, drug addiction was wiped out throughout the country and largely banished from the country for 40 years. But it's now on the rise again.

China is now alerting itself to the research and management of habit-forming medicines, seeing that world-wide misuse of such drugs has greatly impaired the health of patients. . . .Drug addiction is escalating shockingly due in part to the country's promotion of tourism and trade, and infiltration by international drug dealers who are once more looking at China as a lucrative mass market.

Reminiscent of the British opium push?
The press reported 70,000 registered opium smokers and heroin addicts in 1989, mostly young people, and multiplied thousands uncounted.

The dance craze

In April 1989, *Beijing Daily* announced that all dance halls in the city's joint venture hotels would now admit Chinese nationals. In the past, entrance was limited to people holding a foreign or Taiwan passport. "People can now disco to their hearts' content, bringing a great increase in profits from ticket and drink sales."

Break-dancing became a new craze in China, as reported by several Chinese periodicals and many newspapers. *China Reconstructs*, May 1989, reported,

Strolling through Beijing on a warm summer's evening, residents could be forgiven for thinking they were somehow in New York or some other Western city. Shiny new 'ghetto blasters' pound out loud Western music, while fashionably dressed Chinese young men vie with each other to perform the intricate steps of the Electric Boogie. More than a decade after it originated in the U.S., break-dancing has swept the city like a storm. In spite of conservative opposition, it looks as if it's here to stay.

One boy interviewed saw the U.S. movie *Break Dance* 14 times. Many initially feared that the film would cause problems in maintaining public order among the youth, so its release was held back until 1987. Tickets were more expensive than for any other foreign film but thousands flocked to see it. Special gloves, *Nike* sports shoes, and distinctive clothing became the rage.

A feature film entitled *Rock and Roll Youth* was produced by the Beijing Youth Film Studio. A Rock contest in Nanjing lasted 20 days. Each night nearly ten thousand people attended. Such contests across the country began to draw entrants from all walks of life including workers, cadres, middle school and college students, as well as professional dancers. Ballrooms with dim lighting, loud music and a flashing disco ball sprang up around the country.

Beijing Review, March 1989 reported,

The Break-dancing craze among Chinese youngsters is a social reflection of today's lifestyle and cultural psychology. Fans said the dances can make the participants as well as the viewers intensely excited, and at the same time, lighthearted and relaxed. . . .Although many Chinese feel disgusted with break-dancing, most appreciate it or at least maintain a lenient attitude toward such a craze.

And the music goes on. . .

In 1988 China imported more than one million audio tapes and records, a 30 percent rise from the previous year, reported *China Daily*, February 1989. They ranged from classical works to pop songs and disco—3,000 labels in all. In addition, China imported more than 20,000 compact discs valued at more than 100 yuan each. With the improvement of living conditions, more and more Chinese can afford stereo sets, thus increasing the demand for records.

It is not unusual for the concert hall of Zhongshan Park in Beijing to blast with drum beats, echo with the screaming of electro-acoustic guitars, and a clapping, dancing young Chinese audience.

The performer might be someone like the long-haired Cui Jian, a current idol, dressed in baggy military uniform and heavy army boots. Before 1985, most Chinese people had no idea what rock and roll music was. Cui helped to skyrocket it to its present incredible popularity. "It's anti-tradition, anti-culture; it's the ideology of modern man and sometimes a manifestation of the sexual drive," explains Cui. Does that sound familiar?

A survey of the ever-changing tastes of the young consumer in China turned up the unusual popularity of 'jail songs.' A somber, repressive atmosphere is expressed by young criminals behind prison bars. The siren of a police car shrieks, and shackles clank in the background, sometimes to the accompanying moan of wind and storm. A popular film actor, Chi Zhiqiang, committed a crime and was jailed, making such songs even more fashionable. Tapes and videos with jail and prison themes surpassed ten million sales.

Seeking to understand the appeal of such themes, the survey suggested that it is psychological. Some sympathize with the criminal's plight because of their own family experiences. Naive young people are curious about the strange and dismal prison life. Depression, hopelessness, and disillusionment are as common among youth in China as in the West.

Little more than a decade ago, tape recorders were scarce and expensive. Since China opened to the West, they became more available to the Chinese. Listening to pop music, especially from America, has become a favorite pastime. Hits by singers from Hong Kong and Taiwan as well as the West climbed on the Chinese charts. Love themes with strong sexual nuances appealed to Chinese youth who now dare to express their emotions more openly.

Erotica in the media

Book stores and sidewalk book stalls reflect the tastes of new China. According to *Women of China*, October 1988, demand for academic books and classics was severely dropping off. The sale of scientific and technological works shot up. Surveys showed that women college students and career women around 30 to 40 were ardent buyers of anything and everything. Their tastes unleashed, they're quick to buy books on beauty, home economics, education, or health.

Enemies as well as friends are coming through China's new open door. A wave of pornographic magazines and books literally engulfed China, fanned by pornographic videos smuggled through the black market. *China Daily*, March 1989 reported that a decade ago novels with sexual descriptions were not openly available. But today, such books are everywhere in book stalls with eye-catching titles and pictures.

China's State News and Publication Bureau labeled some translations of American best sellers as pornographic and banned them. Such novels were said to "stimulate crime because they describe kidnapping, rape, and how to escape from capture and judicial punishment." China believes that book censorship is still necessary because of China's historical conservativeness in the area of sexual expression. But she is having a hard time deciding on criteria to define what is obscene. The article added, "One frequent consequence of banned books is that they sell most quickly!" The *South China Morning Post*, October 22, 1991, reported that China's Ministry of Culture has called on its officials to go on the offensive in the battle against Western influences in literature and the arts.

"Literary works devoted to violence are on the increase in the Chinese book market and winning a large readership." A Chinese and foreign literature task force in early 1989 sought to understand the phenomenon. The love of violence, some researchers said, has its social background and foundation in every culture. The Chinese tradition for violent literature can be traced to its own classical novels. Descriptions of crime and violence are found in all types of popular fiction, including revolutionary stories.

Of course, the same is true in the West—frontier days, Indian fights, war adventures, and the like. China and the West both struggle with the violence question in its media. One literature expert said,

But the social effect of violence literature is the subject of sharp controversy [anywhere], with one school of thought emphasizing its harmful impact through the readers' imitation of the acts, and another, its [beneficial] role of sublimation, which is thought to help reduce actual crime.

Where did all this lead?

Take a breath. *There's more!* ○

6

Driven Up A Great Wall

As China began to flounder in the uncharted waters of free-enterprise, stumble after trendy capitalist ways, and imitate Western moral pollution, her people understandably became confused. The rapid and drastic flip-flop of standards of conduct are figuratively driving them "up the wall."

Now they're never sure: What is permitted and what is taboo? What the government painted black before, now seems to be whitewashed. And the formerly white, by Communist definition, is now at least dirty gray. The resulting stress and tension are affecting the mental health of young and old in China.

As Christians, we know that the only place to obtain peace of heart and mind is in Jesus Christ. Only there can we find the anchors of life. Let's explore with compassion, understanding, and prayer the condition of China's people as they try to deal with life *without* such a sure answer.

Sowing and reaping

Let's continue to look at what China's own media reported. In a letter to the editor of *China Daily* in April 1989 a reader quoted statistics in only one major city, Tianjin, but they were said to be typical of the situation across the country just before the Tiananmen Square incident.

> Out of 50,000 college students, 16 percent have suffered from anxiety, nervousness, depression or problems due to the unusually early onset of sexual awareness. And in Shanghai, of students from elementary

school to high school age, 27 percent have some kind of emotional disorder, are tired of study, have premature love affairs, smoke in excess, or run away from home. In addition, most are bothered by impulsiveness, envy, worry, or melancholy. Not a small number of students show a sense of inferiority, squeamishness, aggression or strong self-will.

China blames rock music, explicit films, pornographic videos, American television programs, radio, and literature from the West for causing China's youth to express sexual feelings and ideas at a considerably earlier age than their culture ever allowed. The escalation of China's economy and the accompanying acceleration in the pace of life contribute to stirring the muddy waters.

Hard to leave the closet

Most people in China who realize they may have a psychological problem are still reluctant to admit it to anyone else or to consult a psychologist. The basic conservativeness of the Chinese culture and tradition holds them back. Clinical psychology has always been overlooked in China because psychological disorders have not generally been regarded as illness. As a result, the number of people with psychiatric defects has increased.

Beijing's psychologists have set up new consulting services for a whole range of problems. Students and intellectuals make up a large proportion of those who have gone to the center for help. *China Daily*, May 1989, suggested,

Conditioned by their culture and history, Chinese are not used to revealing their feelings in a straightforward way to even their close friends and relatives. Because of this, those with psychological troubles usually find themselves with no one to turn to.

Of those who do go for help, some of the problems they reveal to counselors at the centers are: sexual perversion, day dreaming, exhibitionism, kleptomania, voyeurism, unreasoning fear, frustration, failure in love affairs, and depression. Contradictions between people's characters and professions create stress and mental tension. The generation that went through the "Cultural Revolution" is suffering hangovers from mental and ideological conflicts.

Western ideas of competition are overwhelming the Chinese people who are just emerging from the brainwashing of group thought and group decision making. Formerly, the individual was taught to submerge himself in favor of what would benefit the state.

Large cities have set up telephone counseling as a more discreet and confidential way to answer questions and provide advice. Certain phone numbers are provided for adults, and others for elementary and high school students. A hundred school age children dialed the "hot line" 4015043 on its first day in Beijing. Problems discussed were appearance, friendships, love affairs, relationships with parents and teachers, and teen pregnancy.

The *South China Morning Post* July 27, 1991 reported that more than 20,000 anxious Beijing teenagers called China's first teen hot line since February 1989 when it set up its single telephone to serve a city of 10 million. Thirty volunteers anonymously work in shifts to field questions about sex, pregnancy, suicide, parental abuse, and individual rights. The service is available every day after school and on weekends.

A quick way out

Directly related to mental instability, and of course spiritual emptiness, is the tendency to suicide. *China Daily*, March 1989 reported,

> Experts point out that suicide has become the No.1 killer in abnormal deaths in China. It used to be a taboo in China even to study suicide. Yet in recent years we are increasingly haunted by this rising problem. A suicide prevention and treatment center was started in Guangzhou in 1988, the first in all of China and a harbinger of things to come.

About 140,000 people are killing themselves in China every year, and women, especially in the countryside, make up 70 percent.

Group suicides are becoming common. Statistics show that half of the women killed themselves because of family disputes and failures in marriages. Because Chinese men are accustomed to be domineering in family life, the psychological and emotional needs of their wives are often ignored. The above article continued,

> Another important cause of increasing suicide is the great change in our society. Industrialization brings a faster pace and there is conflict between the old and new social values and moral standards. Women, especially, cannot adjust to the changes....As rural women leave their poverty-stricken villages to work in big cities, the contrast is too much for them. Poison and sleeping pills, hanging, diving into water, or jumping off high buildings are the most common methods of suicide.

Till law do us part

Family instability in the midst of China's drastic changes is contributing to mental instability and vice versa. Many young Chinese couples are marrying quickly and now divorcing with ease, reported an article in April 1989, *China Daily*. In large cities the divorce rate is especially alarming.

> In the time it takes for 100 urban couples in fancy Western wedding gowns and tuxedos to go to a studio to have wedding photos taken, 30 couples in that same city go to the county or civil affairs departments to register for divorce. Many of those seeking divorce have been married for only one or two years.

In Beijing alone, 500,000 couples divorced in 1987. An increase in extra-marital affairs contributes to the divorce rate. China's new Criminal Law canceled the regulation against adultery, imitating the law systems of Western countries, and "more adultery has been reported since then, causing many divorces," stated the newspaper.

A professor from the Beijing Institute of Political Science and Law commented that any major social change will inevitably cause the re-organization of families. He said the divorce rate in China began to climb after the chaotic ten years of the "Cultural Revolution."

Art unveiled

Nude art in China? Inconceivable! *Beijing Review*, January 1989, reported an exhibition on the art of the nude created by Chinese painters in Beijing at the China Art Gallery.

The exhibition gave the public a look at a theme long considered 'unhealthy' and obscene in China. The show ran several weeks and featured 136 paintings, the work of 28 young teachers from Beijing's Central Academy of Fine Arts. It was considered a major breakthrough in overcoming the strictures of feudal ideology and traditional culture.

Ten thousand tickets were sold on the first Sunday of the show. Heretofore, art involving the naked body was strictly prohibited in public by the Chinese government. Only one female artist presented her work, and only one male nude painting, a self-portrait, was exhibited. Art forms were mainly classical European, others were naturalistic, and a few were clearly expressionist. Some were abstract and distorted, others realistic. A Chinese senior artist and professor commented,

When I was a student, the drawing of nudes was obligatory and commonplace. It has only become a problem since the 1950s, when people declared that all depiction of nudes were decadent. Such attitudes are connected with the feudal tradition running through Chinese culture.

A Chinese art critic agreed.

It would have been impossible to hold this exhibition without the atmosphere generated by China's reform and open policy. It reflects progress in China, and will undoubtedly have a marked effect on the development of aesthetic appreciation among Chinese citizens.

As it does in the West?

Where have all the craftsmen gone?

An Associated Press feature appeared in American newspapers in early January 1992 titled, "Traditional Chinese Art is Losing Modern Race." It pointed out,

> Craftsmen at the Beijing Folk Musical Instruments Factory lovingly shape fine wood and snake skin into traditional stringed instruments and drums. But what keeps the factory going are electric guitars and modern metal drum sets. Not just in music but across the art scene, traditional forms are losing ground to modern, Western forms. Pop songs, videotaped adventure movies, televised soap operas and oil paintings are drawing interest away from folk tunes, historical costume dramas and pen-and-ink drawings of mountains wreathed in fog. Past official policies are blamed for contributing to the shift...particularly the Mao-inspired turmoil of the 1966-76 Cultural Revolution. Most young people prefer a night at the disco to an evening at the Beijing Opera...which they label as 'too old-fashioned.'

May I have a light?

We were told repeatedly by Chinese friends in our travels there that most people in China smoke because they are nervous and mentally agitated. The availability of Western cigarettes has not helped the addiction.

"Over the last few years, famous brands of foreign cigarettes have appeared on sale in every part of China in quantities previously hard to imagine" reported *Guangming Ribao*, (Guangming Daily).

50

Does the government of China spend so much on something that it knows will damage her people's health?

Not necessarily. The newspaper reported that foreign cigarettes are sold in China on consignment. China provides foreign businessmen with docks, storehouses, and counters, running no risks and gaining millions of yuan in foreign exchange. It's a cushy job.

While the number of smokers in Britain and the U.S. has dropped 30 percent in the past 10 years, mostly because of health awareness, both of those countries have been successful in opening new markets in developing countries. (*We* don't want lung cancer but it's okay for *others*?)

A World Health Organization official pointed out that by sponsoring Chinese acrobatic and sports activities, several foreign tobacco companies have skillfully promoted greater smoking in China. Once their brands have become well known, they rapidly dump large quantities of their goods on the market. Two Chinese companies have signed a U.S. $21 million agreement with America's R.J.Reynolds Tobacco Intl. to manufacture Camels, Winstons, and two other brands of cigarettes in Xiamen, China.

In the 400 years since tobacco was introduced into China, the Chinese have become the world's greatest smokers, according to *China Daily*, April 1989.

Of China's urban residents over the age of 15, 40 percent are smokers. Seventy-four percent of China's smokers recognize the hazards of smoking but continue the habit regardless, even referring to cigarettes as 'coffin nails'. Despite escalating prices of popular brand-name cigarettes, smokers would rather spend their money on tobacco than on books or newspapers.

In Nanjing alone, 30 percent of the students at secondary schools are regular smokers—a 300 percent rise in two years. A significant percent began smoking before they were 13 years old. *China Daily*, May 1989, reported,

Youngsters today are often seen smoking in cinemas and cafes or even near campuses; smoking is perceived by them as a way of acting 'cool and grown-up' before

51

their peers. Foreign cigarettes indicate a higher social status. They are hoarded by speculators as rare commodities and used by smart young things and upstarts to flaunt their wealth.

Smoking among juveniles is often disregarded by Chinese parents who sometimes actually give their children money to buy cigarettes. The articles above said that scenes showing glamorous actors and actresses smoking in films and on television made the habit look sophisticated, adult, and attractive to impressionable youngsters.

You've come a long way, baby

China Daily, April 1989 reported,

More and more Chinese women are joining the ranks of an estimated 240 million smokers in China. In traditional China, smoking by women was usually associated with rural women and regarded as something indecent or uncivilized. Today, smoking among young women in urban areas is becoming fashionable. Many women regard smoking as an act of defiance against tradition and an expression of modern civilization—even a challenge to the male dominant society, and a demonstration of their new equal rights. One junior high school student admitted that eight out of 25 girls in her class smoked secretly, imitating 'pretty girls in foreign movies who have cigarettes dangling from their lips.'

Declining work ethic

Mental and societal instability influences the work ethic. In China today people say that many have nothing to do, while there is much work that people are unwilling to do.

Surprisingly, this phenomenon is still spreading in China in spite of the new direction of private enterprise. It is now compounded by the reversion to central government planning of the hard line leadership and resulting unemployment. On the one hand, the country has about 20 million redundant personnel because workers in state enterprises are not fired despite their low efficiency. On the other hand, some trades in urban areas have about 30 million vacant positions. *Ban Yue Tan* (Fortnightly Forum) October 1988 reported,

> In the past few years, although more than 15 million farmers have entered the cities and work there, positions still remain vacant. In some work units people squander their time and do nothing. During work hours, they chat with fellow workers, play chess and cards or watch television. In some places, two people are responsible for sweeping the same floor, and six women look after three children in the factory nursery.

People are somewhat more free to choose their jobs now. Workers are desperately needed in the low-paid textile, machinery, and sanitation industries, but workers have become extremely picky and shy away from such jobs. In recent years, university and college students have become unwilling to work in grassroots units because the "serve the people" motivation has been replaced by a "line your own pocket" work ethic. Teachers, professors, and other intellectuals, because of the poor pay scale, are leaving schools to go into business.

In 1989 China had an additional 10 million people looking for work, of whom only 5 million were guaranteed employment by the State, according to government sources quoted in *China Daily*, May 1989. This raised the unemployment rate to 3.5 percent if the remainder were unable to find jobs on their own. Most new job seekers are recent school graduates, demobilized servicemen, farmers transferring to industries, and workers who lost their jobs in many enterprises where staff was cut to optimize productivity.

The bottom line

The West, the "free world," the democratic nations, or ourselves as Christians from materialistic countries should not climb on our high horses or be "pots calling the kettle black." In the West our freedoms have also resulted in license, the morals of our society have deteriorated, crime is rampant, and we have also plunged down the abyss of corruption on nearly every level. *We* could echo all the ills of present Chinese society—*and more.*

Actually, the decline of moral standards is not because of China's system of government. "The heart is desperately wicked and deceitful above all things," the Bible says, whether a person lives under a democratic or an autocratic system. A person is just as empty, restless, and dissatisfied in any culture or under any political structure, whether it is sugar-coated with idealism, patriotism, or expressed in an undisguised lust for things. The solution, which we shall discuss more in detail in a later chapter, is not to export our exact form of democracy to China, but to exalt and offer Christ, regardless of what political system is in place.

Jesus only, with His peace, is the answer to the pressures and stresses of life's changing scene—whether in China or the West. ○

7

To Market, To Market

In this chapter let us take a closer look at China's push toward the "Four Modernizations" so that we may understand her developing economy. We'll see how her people were caught in the squeeze of paradoxes. During the eighties, instead of the patriotic, Marxist, and revolutionary slogans that we saw in the seventies, we were amazed to see advertisements and enticements for commodities and luxury items splashed on huge billboards. Such consumer advertising had been taboo. In driving down a new road to economic progress, China was beginning to push her foot hard on the accelerator.

Her "Four Modernizations" program was her golden key to enter the door of the world market with status and influence. The four areas of modernization are agriculture, industry, science-technology, and defense.

China is pragmatic

To thrust forward her drive for the "Four Modernizations" China's initial scheme was to invite foreign specialists, professional persons, business executives, and firms to supervise projects in China, to cooperate in joint ventures, and thus develop China's trade with the world market. For the time being, China obviously put her economic progress and national welfare ahead of ideological differences with those she had labeled "barbarians" in the past.

China opened her own door voluntarily from the inside. The outside world, like the big bad wolf in the children's story, didn't need to "huff and puff to blow the house down." The West didn't have to force its way into China with gunboats or military persuasion. China was enticed by her own lusts (James 1:14).

The difference in China's relationship with foreigners at this point in history is that she has *invited* the West to do business *on China's own terms*. We've seen that China insists on being taken seriously as the equal of other nations. She will no longer allow other nations to humiliate and exploit her.

Small private enterprise shops began to spring up everywhere. Peasants were no longer required to sell their produce exclusively to the state. The government allowed them to plant and market some crops of their own choice. Some people began to prosper beyond their wildest dreams. Joint ventures with the West resulted in a flirtation with Western-style management techniques—a far cry from Marxism.

Communist private enterprise?

What was the nature of the private enterprise that China tolerated and encouraged in the eighties? Her Ministry of Finance issued definitive "Interim Regulations on Private Enterprises of the People's Republic of China." The first few Articles of Chapter 1: General Provisions, stated:

> These regulations are formulated for the purpose of encouraging and guiding the healthy development of private enterprises, protecting the lawful rights and interests of private enterprises, strengthening supervision and administration, and promoting the development of the socialist planned commodity economy.' Private enterprise,' for the purposes of these interim regulations, means those economic organizations whose assets are owned by individuals and which have eight or more employees and are intended to be profit-making enterprises. A private economy complements the socialist public ownership economy. The state protects the lawful rights and interests of private enterprises. All the operating activities of a private enterprise shall comply with provisions of national laws, regulations and policies.

Prior to the June 1989 catastrophe, statistics showed that 115,000 registered private enterprises had already mushroomed in the country, with 1,847,000 employees. Add to that more than 50,000 collectives and over 60,000 cooperative enterprises, which in management are private. During a short period China had developed 225,000 private enterprises with 3,670,000 employees. If the 14,130,000 individuals who were in business for themselves are counted, China had almost 26 million employees in private enterprises!

The people took their government at its word, before it changed its mind, and ran down the field with the idea of private enterprise.

Back to square one

Why should China suddenly allow such economic freedom? In fact, private enterprise is really nothing new for China. Chinese people have always been individually enterprising in business. State control *was new* to them. Their government suddenly forced them to concede state ownership of everything, including property they had long considered their own. The Communist regime imposed it upon them under the guise of being "for the people's benefit." Historically, the Chinese have always been shrewd in business at every level at home and abroad. Chinese people scattered throughout the world have the reputation of being highly motivated, hard working, intelligent entrepreneurs.

Jingjixue Zhoubao (Economic Weekly) highlighted some of the characteristics of current private enterprises in China:

> High efficiency, a steady work rhythm and a full load have become major features of labor productivity in private enterprises. In terms of production and management, the private sector lays more emphasis on economic returns from investment and uses it as the yardstick for enterprise production and management. Both bosses and employees are hard-working and thrifty to a level no state-run enterprise can compare with. The private sector has a far better approach to serving its customers. Many private enterprises have adopted the principle of 'customers first' to attract business. . . .A hire system is used. . .and stress is laid on the laws of value and market demand, the concern being mainly to make profits. . . .Private enterprises can boldly implement new plans, blaze new trails, and

shoulder greater risks. [The system] caters to improving people's lives, provides funds for state finance, and stimulates the development of the state economy. . . .

Considering the poor service, indifferent attitudes, and lack of motivation shown by China's employees in state-run enterprises in the early years, this had to be a fresh breeze blowing through the bamboo groves. In state-run enterprises the wages of workers had not been linked with good performance.

Isn't it amazing what happens to an individual in any society when he sees the possibility of *lining his own pocket* while the enterprise he works for makes a profit? He no longer complains about hard work and longer hours!

How it works on the streets

When free enterprise was permitted again in China, it was first expressed by sidewalk or street-side markets where farmers spread their produce on the ground for sale—fruit, vegetables, and the like. Then came rough tables with canopies, followed by more substantial stalls where they displayed clothing, shoes, Chinese arts and crafts, household necessities—anything that could be obtained wholesale or that individuals could produce or hand craft themselves. The assortment of goods varied day by day. Fresh fish, live poultry, raw meat, and all kinds of ready-cooked food continue to be the mainstay of daily small businesses for which demand will never cease. The Chinese call such self-employed individuals *getihu*. These are a flashback to small time Chinese entrepreneurs common throughout China's long history, who were curtailed during revolutionary days.

One young owner of a stall on Xiushui East street market in Beijing offered, "I admire all the rich people in the world because I consider money to be a symbol of success." According to a story in the *Beijing Review*, after only 18 months of self-employed hard work, that particular young man had earned enough money to invest the equivalent of U.S. $40,300 in an electrical appliance processing factory being built in the suburbs of Beijing. With a U.S. $10,000 investment later in the year he planned to open another stand elsewhere in the city to sell garments. "I hope to invest in foreign countries someday," he said with a confident smile.

59

Certainly this man is not be typical of *getihu* but exemplifies that such private profits are becoming possible. Let's not forget that *only a comparatively few* Chinese are getting rich. Over 70 million people still live in poverty, some with an annual income of less than 200 yuan (U.S.$53).

Can *Communists* become millionaires?

Xu Jizhu, 45, the director of the Shendong Metal Materials Factory near Shenyang owns a business worth at least 8 million yuan (U.S. $2.1 million). He was accepted as a probationary Communist Party member in December 1988 by the village Party branch and approved by the Township Party Committee. A high official stated that since Xu "believes in Communism," his wealth should not exclude him from the Party. But other Party organizations are still debating whether it's *appropriate* for millionaires to become members of the Party. Millionaires in the past have been automatically linked to exploitation of workers.

How does Xu justify his wealth in a socialist society? He provides jobs for 300 workers. He made the government happy by paying 1.9 million yuan in taxes for the past three years. His factory earned $400,000 from exports the previous year. He donated 200,000 yuan toward his village's primary school and a water project. He started a welfare workshop solely for the benefit of 70 handicapped people. The following year he expected to become a full voting member of the Party.

Truly a new day dawned in China! Larger and more complex enterprises, small companies, industries, factories, businesses for almost any commodity, product, or service began to spring up and were privately owned. But fearful that their good fortune possibly might not last, people at the grass-roots hurried to make money and buy up consumer goods. Was it a premonition?

Changes at the grass-roots

Communism considered golf a totally capitalistic vice during revolutionary days in China. Now Chinese on official levels are becoming expert at the sport, and the government encourages the building of modern golf courses for the elite.

Local Chinese, for whom three nights in a world class hotel would equal their annual salary, often take their families into hotel lobbies and proudly take photos in luxurious settings.

Families pay for photos of themselves posed sitting in a fancy car in a parking lot or beside a motorcycle owned by someone else. Owning a car is still only a dream for the average citizen because automobiles have been reserved for government officials and foreigners. Moreover, streets would be impassable if private car ownership mushroomed.

Young Chinese rock music stars make fabulous salaries, and we have seen that they sometimes try to escape income taxes.

Many farmers have become part of a new capitalist class and are role models for young Chinese who now see dollar signs in "staying down on the farm."

The children of top Communist party officials enjoy incredible privileges and status, are never short of money, and are often sent abroad to the most expensive schools.

Fashion shows by girls who were formerly factory workers are popular. Interviewed, most of them said they don't care about politics; only their own lives are important to them.

During the Cultural Revolution Chinese capitalist businessmen were relegated to demeaning work as common laborers in factories they previously owned. Or they were sent to the countryside to work with the peasants. Of those who survived, many are now being "rehabilitated" by the government and put in charge of big business again.

Justifying capitalism

In the early stages of his economic reforms, Deng declared that "to get rich is glorious." He admitted that some will get rich sooner than others, but they could be role models. The Chinese people, dazed and confused, were jubilant with the change in policy from the "rich is dirty" revolutionary years.

Zhao Yao, professor of the Scientific Socialism Teaching and Research Section of the CCP Central Committee's Party School, included the United States in his explanation of China's changing identity:

61

In the face of the enormous scientific and technological revolution of the last few decades, both socialism and capitalism are undergoing great changes. Effectively, both systems are in a stage of transition, from traditional to modern capitalism and from traditional to modern socialism. These are tremendous changes marking important stages of history.

Having espoused Communism, China recklessly traveled the radical revolutionary road until she nearly committed suicide. Now she has apparently crossed the median strip to proceed in the opposite direction—or so it seems. We have seen that some of her more progressive and pragmatic leaders initiated a decade of incredible economic reforms. Such reforms challenged pure Marxist principles, increased incomes, and opened fantastic social and economic doors. Such action understandably shook up and angered old Party leadership who felt threatened with the loss of their authoritarian control and privileged positions.

Hang on to the pendulum

The Chinese people, hanging precariously to the swinging pendulum, are still not sure which direction to trust. At first their leaders forced them to *shout against* capitalism under Mao Zedong; then for a decade *encouraged* what is being called "street capitalism." But during and after the 1989 Tiananmen Massacre, the government used the same bloody military tactics of the Cultural Revolution that it had only recently repudiated.

China's leaders told their people that the West is *bad;* then for a decade or so, it was *good*—now *bad again*? Private ownership was *dirty* and now it is not only *clean* but encouraged. Profit was *unpatriotic*—now it is *legitimate*? To imitate the Americans was *decadent*, then it became *acceptable*—now contact with Westerners is *suspicious* again!

While this book was being written, China's progress flowing in a more moderate direction reversed itself again. The softer line hardened. The recent *white* was *black* once more; the *good* that the people were growing accustomed to was branded *bad* again. The push-pull of political vacillation and Party squabble once again has made China's people dizzy—and is baffling the rest of the world.

During the first draft of this chapter, the smiling, handshaking visit of Gorbachev to Beijing was supposedly creating a new climate to "restore friendship and normalize relations" between the *bear* and the *dragon*. During the final draft, the Soviet Union had already crumbled and the bear was slinking away, dazed and confused about its identity and without a "den" to call its own.

And what will China and the world be like when the reader looks at these pages?

Press on with me in the next chapter as we try to analyze what constitutes "the good life" for the people of China and *for ourselves*— and what God has to say about it. ○

8

Prosperity Is A "Hot Potato"

As we have seen, a temporary fresh breeze began to blow across China more than a decade ago. Her Marxist leadership loosened the reins of total state ownership to allow some private enterprise and a modified form of capitalism. The front door, back door, and side doors were opening to the outside world at last.

The people blinked with skepticism briefly, then "took off like a shot" for the Chinese version of "the good life." With some coveted discretionary income finally available, people rushed to buy commodities that had been denied during the austerity of the Mao era with its contempt for bourgeois values and private ownership.

"Most wanted" list

Early on, eight items, give or take, represented their idea of a "good life": a sewing machine, a black unisex bicycle, a simple camera, a radio, an ordinary watch, a tape player, a black and white TV, and an electric fan. Do we find that amusing?

In the years that followed, China began to enjoy what, for her people, was a surge of prosperity: industries boomed, trade with the world thrived, joint business ventures with the West prospered, private enterprises flourished. The economic picture changed from black and white to color. So did the wants and tastes of China's people. Economic growth parallels the desires of consumers.

Forget the sewing machine! (But put your Mao jackets and baggy trousers in moth balls—you may one day be forced to wear them again!) Bring on ready-made garments in the latest American fashions to go with the disco and break-dancing craze. Faded blue jeans, jackets, and skirts have become a permanent fad. With designer labels, of course! Bicycles sport flashy colors in American models. Motor bikes and motorcycles loaded with fancy gadgets roar down China's streets weaving in and out among the millions of bicycles.

Color TV sets are a status symbol even though a laborer may have to work 6 months to pay for one. A remote control is a "must" although most places receive only two channels! The latest model stereos with enormous speakers are the rage. Record albums feature American, Hong Kong, yes, even rock stars from Taiwan. VCRs and videos are hot imports. Nothing less than Seiko or Rolex watches will do. Refrigerators, automatic washers, telephones, and air conditioners are high on the list. Scrap the typewriter—bring on the personal computer!

Self-examination

Do we have any right to point an accusing finger at the sudden pursuit of material goods by China's people? The materialism of our Western world, especially of the United States, can hardly be matched anywhere. The more we feel "at home" when we travel in China— enjoying the luxuries to which we are accustomed, staying in world class hotels, paying with credit cards—the more we can see the devil's strategy.

Satan has done his infernal best in the Western world to woo men and women away from spiritual values through giving them a push toward materialistic pursuits; he has sedated us with affluence. Why should we "set our affection on things above, not on things of this earth" if we are already enjoying everything we want now?

The "prince of this world" is now trying out his new prosperity tactic on the 1.1 billion citizens of China. The late esteemed Chinese pastor Wang Mingdao, who suffered 23 years in prison for his faith, declared upon his release that he feared materialism and prosperity among Christians more than persecution and suffering.

What nourishes spirituality?

It's strange but true, and not a comforting thought, that God's people grow stronger through trouble not blessings. It's more difficult to be a Christian in times of prosperity. During opposition or persecution, life is more simple: we must choose whether to stand for Christ or deny Him. Black is black and white is white. Survival is at stake. We draw closer to God because He is the only one left to call on for our needs. In times of prosperity we are too placid and cozy. We don't need God because we are self-sufficient. We begin by neglecting God, then we forget Him.

Most people don't seem to know how to handle prosperity well—Christians included. If God blesses us, we still aren't satisfied. If we have a little, we want more. If we have something good, we want something better. If we have something small, we nevertheless want something bigger. Adequate things give place to desires for newer, more fashionable items, later models.

China's drive to modernize and catch up with the world was, of course, materialistic and needed to accommodate capitalism with its incentive for private profit. The leadership tried hard to squeeze such concepts under the Communist umbrella while retaining a high degree of state ownership and control over the people. Marxism, often thought of in terms of idealism, has at the same time always been materialistic because its whole scenario begins and ends with life on this planet. In its view, man is only an animal evolving upward with society, which is struggling toward a utopia on earth.

Where has all the seeking gone?

An evangelical leader in the West assessed the race for materialism in China: *"Gone is the great spiritual seeking* they have been famous for [during the Mao era]. Mao's visions of building a new man have vanished, to be replaced by a frantic race for money."

If we take a magnifying glass and look carefully at the grassroots people in China, we may find that what some perceived as a "great spiritual seeking" during the heyday of the Communist revolution was still motivated by materialistic concerns common to mankind. Yes, it had a veneer of idealism and patriotism, but the regime promised people "a better life" *materially* after class distinctions were erased and everything would be divided more equitably.

Communism rolled into China not on wheels of "pie in the sky," as Christianity was accused of promising for the hereafter, but "more rice in your bowl—soon." The present race for material goods is *nothing new*, simply an extension of that desire. Communism did *not* fill that bowl *or* the spiritual void; it brought only the hot air of "promises-promises."

China attempted during the eighties to experiment with modified capitalism or free enterprise. China's people hoped that the experiment would not only fill their bowls, but provide a refrigerator in which to store the leftover rice and abundant food. And then a better apartment in which to keep the refrigerator—and a color television in the apartment—and a motor bike to replace their bicycle—on and on. Whatever our culture or political system, materialism can never satisfy us because *nothing is ever enough.*

But "the great spiritual seeking" is not gone. A young Chinese Christian who joined the Tiananmen student demonstrations prior to the Beijing massacre was quoted in *News Network International,* "The students are not only calling for democracy. Underneath they are crying for real meaning in life." He explained that the mundane materialism offered by Deng Xiaoping had backfired.

> People are starting to say, 'Is this all we have to live for: a bigger television or a better refrigerator?' Chinese people need something more important to live for. We are not natural materialists. Now that Mao's vision is defunct and Deng's has been rejected, I am hopeful that many will come to Christ, whose vision is the greatest and most eternal in scope.

Do we Christians in the West have as clear a perspective on materialism in our society and our personal lives as this student expressed?

Man's heart is restless until it finds its rest and fulfillment in Christ—for Whom the heart was created by God. Material things won't satisfy Chinese hearts any more than they satisfy the hearts of people in the West or anywhere else in the world. Not only will they not satisfy, *they will corrupt.*

Our response is the key

Does the Bible teach that every Christian must adopt a Spartan lifestyle and refuse the benefits that technological and scientific progress are bringing? Is there something intrinsically more spiritual about poverty, suffering, and oppression that makes us better Christians? If we have plenty, must that toll the decline of our spiritual lives? Isn't it *our reaction or response* to either of these conditions that determines our relationship with God and His pleasure in us? And limits or expands our effectiveness in witness, whether cross-culturally or down the block?

Material things are neutral. The dictionary defines a materialist as "a person who gives attention to or emphasizes material objects, needs, and considerations, *with a disinterest in or rejection of spiritual values.*" Therefore a materialist can be either rich or poor. Christians who are in want or who have plenty are to give priority to spiritual and eternal values.

The apostle Paul admitted that the ability to handle either plenty or want was a secret and had to be learned.

> . . .I have learned to be content in whatever circum-
> stances I am. I know how to get along with humble
> means, and I also know how to live in prosperity; in any
> and every circumstance I have learned the secret of
> being filled and going hungry, both of having abun-
> dance and suffering need. I can do all things through
> Him who strengthens me (Phil. 4:11-13).

How then shall we live?

Although dizzy from swinging on the political and economic pendulum, some of the people of China have begun enjoying what is still a meager measure of economic prosperity and consumer goods. Would we deny them that opportunity if we don't deny it to ourselves?

As Christians in the West, whether we have opportunities to travel, work, teach, or study in China, or whether we hope for meaningful encounters with Chinese students, scholars, and immigrant families in our own country, we cannot hide our own priorities regarding materialism or things eternal. Let's be sure *our* priorities are in line with the biblical perspective and that we practice what we preach. O

9

The Tiananmen Square Affair

During the latter part of April 1989 and culminating on May 4, which was the 70th anniversary of China's *first* student movement for democracy, hundreds of thousands of Chinese students converged on Tiananmen Square in Beijing and began boldly demonstrating "for democracy and against corruption in government."

But as their demonstrations gathered momentum, elsewhere on that very Square on China's major annual holiday, May Day 1989, 10,000 new recruits of the Communist Youth League in Beijing took oaths in a mass rally. That represented still entrenched Marxist training of youth.

But the excitement of the students mounted when they saw what looked like a good omen for "their side," a startling change quietly taking place in the decoration of Tiananmen Square. The large portraits of Marx, Engels, Lenin and Stalin disappeared! Only portraits of Dr. Sun Yat-sen and Mao Zedong remained. Dr. Sun, proclaimed as the "George Washington of China" by both Communists and the government in Taiwan, founded the Republic of China in 1911 and was not a Communist.

At least on the surface, the student demonstrators didn't plan to topple the Communist system. They were only asking for more moderate leadership sympathetic to the needs of the people, the elimination of corruption at the leadership level, and more freedom *within the system*. But it was an unrealistic dream to try to make Communism work better or to purify it. At the very heart of it lies totalitarian control over every aspect of the lives of its citizens. China isn't a *"people's republic"*; the *state* holds absolute power.

The seeds for the student demonstrations were reported to have

71

been sown at Peoples' University in Beijing, the institution attended by the children of the elite, of the high officials, and of government leaders. Those involved in the demonstrations were the cream of the crop, the committed, dedicated youth who could have been leaders of China in the future. Many lost their lives when the army was turned loose against them by their elders.

The student demonstrations escalated. Few thought that the enthusiastic, peaceful, open-hearted, spirited jolly student demonstrations for democracy would soon result in such a tragic waste of life and an economic and national catastrophe.

Like prairie fire, the momentum that the students started was taken up by millions of ordinary people throughout China, in Hong Kong, and in major cities worldwide. In the eyes of China's leaders, it got completely out-of-hand.

The fuse is lit

The world had been wondering in May 1989: Is China still Communist? Is she socialist? Is she borderline capitalist? How much reform can this awakening giant stand? Will the hard line Party members be forced to go along with such highly visible and daring pro-democracy rumblings and lose their positions and perks (the many luxuries they were enjoying in such an un-Marxist fashion)? Would they put up with the flood of out-of-control reforms implemented by the soft liners?

Or would they reach "a last straw" and attempt to crack down in desperation and possibly bloody confrontation in a bid to retain power? We didn't have to wait long to find out.

China's Communist regime does *not* permit public demonstrations for democracy, or the building of a "goddess of liberty" under the very nose of the giant portrait of Chairman Mao as it hung overlooking Tiananmen Square. Shouts of "Down with the government's leaders" are prohibited by China's Constitution.

The issue became one of political control and national reputation. After a brief calm before the storm, the elderly Communist Party hard liners, the ultra-conservative Marxists, wrestled the wheel away from the soft liners and made an overheated decision.

The great leap backward

While the world held its breath and watched the unfolding of the incredible tragic drama on worldwide television, tanks rolled in, shots were fired, blood flowed, bodies were crushed, youth of promise by the thousands perished.

Deng Xiaoping was undoubtedly still the man with his finger on the final trigger. He was the same leader who had declared to his people and to the outside world that there was no turning back from his policy of economic reforms. "If the policy is correct, if it is right for the people, if it improves their lot, the people will understand and continue to pursue the reforms."

Deng had been hailed as a hero, the pacesetter who took China from the fanatic Mao era into the community of nations. China's world-popular leader, the man of the hour, America's acclaimed "Man of the Year" had indeed begun to provide Chinese citizens with certain economic reforms. They cheered in the equivalent of "Happy Days are here (or at least coming) again!" Suddenly the world was calling him the "Butcher of Beijing." His image seemed now as marred with chaotic decisions and cruel actions as Mao's was in his final days. As some protesters threw ink on the portrait of Mao in Tiananmen Square during the demonstrations, so blood was on the face and hands of Deng before he would inevitably step off the power stage in China. (But the Chinese have a saying, "Not until the final nail is driven into the coffin do we know a man's true character." *Anything* could still happen.)

The government explained its drastic actions as "a lesson for the people." What lesson? That *political* freedom is *not included* in any economic reform package. And that opposition to the existing government still constitutes counter-revolutionary action. The people realized that they were still behind bars, though somewhat better off economically. A well-fed, adequately clothed prisoner is still a prisoner. He longs for *real freedom*. The people, especially the students and intellectuals, wanted *political freedoms* too.

China took a great leap backward—back to Cultural Revolution tactics—and worse, according to Chinese people who are in the midst of a new holocaust. Contrary to what most Chinese on the street thought possible, their government revived out-dated revolutionary slogans, compulsory political indoctrination meetings, and surveillance of the private actions of her people, especially university students and faculty. Once again the government required people to spy on and to accuse one another, and to turn in dissidents and counter-revolutionaries. China's bloody dictatorial grip, which the outside world thought she had put into mothballs along with Mao jackets and caps, was around the necks of her people again.

The Chinese government had assumed a friendship demeanor toward the West only to obtain what China desperately needed economically, technologically, and scientifically. But the Western "carriers" who brought them had also *infected* China's people with contagious ideas of more freedoms and democracy—whatever that meant. The students and intellectuals zealously embraced these new ideas and began to act as if they already *had* them. But they didn't—they were on "fantasy island."

Is there life after Tiananmen?

In the aftermath of the political crackdown, reforms that were barely implemented became unreformed, and the people staggered again under an ailing, overheated economy. Runaway inflation led to a two-year-plus moratorium on new reforms. The beleaguered people began to suffer again under an austerity program aimed at reducing the inflation rate and slowing industrial growth.

People gazed discouraged and disillusioned upon economic stagnation resulting from the hard line government that reverted to Marxist-style central planning. China's media admitted that millions of workers were laid off, unemployment rose, and the living standard declined. Low efficiency, low quality products, and misuse of resources caused increasing stockpiles. Government enterprises were over-staffed and discipline was poor. Materials and energy were wasted and equipment was deteriorating. Foreign exchange revenues dropped and joint ventures started going sour. Literally overnight, China's credibility with the international community took a plunge.

Behind the crackdown curtain

The crackdown on protesters by the military swept across all China from major cities to the countryside. It is almost impossible to maintain anonymity in China. The network of surveillance is like a dragnet. We must remember that China is a police state. Computers are now employed to monitor the activities of all citizens. There's really no place to hide in the long run because the government puts pressure on citizens to turn each other in. This was the case in past revolutionary days, but to the casual observer during the past decade or so of seemingly free coming and going, that era seemed to be fading. The present crackdown proved that the dragnet is alive and well.

The movements and activities of every individual are known, incredible as that may seem in a country of more than a billion people. Each block has its neighborhood "responsible person" who knows each member of every family and keeps tab on them. The ratio of surveillance is one such person to 10 citizens, and ultimately 1 to 3 at the grass-roots level. In many districts the government has made a deal with certain law breakers allowing them freedom in exchange for spying and reporting on their own people. The elderly and retired are enlisted to keep an eye on their own families and neighborhoods. Casual gossip/information is an integral form of this low level communication system.

As a result, protesters and dissidents were brought to mock trials and sentenced—some to death, some to prison, some to labor camp. The *China News Service* reported in April 1991 that in a throwback to the days of Chairman Mao, half of the nation's 2.2 million university students were ordered to go to the villages to "learn from the masses." This largest campaign of "socialist education" since the Cultural Revolution was part of a plan by the Communist Party to wean the people off "bourgeois liberalization." The freedom movement had to go underground again as it did in the past, but it has no intention of dying out. It will rise again, as it has throughout China's history.

Perhaps the majority of China's people never knew what really happened at Tiananmen unless they had access to foreign media. Thought control is still a powerful tool even in the countryside where village loudspeakers continue to blare censored news and whatever propaganda the government wants the people to hear. A blanket of conformity not only stifles free expression but distorts the facts of any event to suit the government's purpose.

What next?

China's political future is uncertain. She seems to run first to one end of the field and then the other, confused as to which is her goal line. We sit in the bleachers and watch the serious un-game and puzzle over the secret huddles and the leadership power struggles. We agonize over a billion people jerked first one way and then another, most of them still grappling with the harsh realities of day-to-day survival.

Just when we think we know China's new stance, it changes. May we be faithful and steadfast in prayer for her people, asking God to give us understanding and discernment to know how to relate for the sake of the witness of Christ in China.

Repercussions for China's Church

How did the events at Tiananmen, the dragnet, and crackdown on protesters affect Christians in China?

Whether or not China's Christians were involved in the freedom demonstrations that precipitated the shocking bloodbath, (and most of them were not) it was almost inevitable that they would suffer renewed persecution, arrest, imprisonment—and worse.

The government typically and indiscriminately branded all protesters, demonstrators, and dissidents as counter-revolutionaries, a label tantamount to treason. Despite a degree of religious tolerance in recent years, Christianity continues to be painted with a foreign or Western brush by China's Marxist and atheist leadership. Many of the estimated 50 million Christians, especially those in the house churches, were again considered criminals and became innocent targets of the crackdown.

China's Christians, however, don't think it strange to suffer as criminals. Didn't the apostle Paul testify of himself,

> Remember Jesus Christ, risen from the dead. . .according to my gospel, for which I suffer hardship even to imprisonment as a criminal; but the word of God is not imprisoned (2 Tim. 2:8,9).

You can count on it: each time a hard line leadership takes control after a high-level power struggle within China's government, even during this past decade of near-capitalist reforms and openness to the outside world, Christians have suffered simply by being part of the general population. But the government has repeatedly taken special advantage of such repressive campaigns to thin out the ranks of Christians. But it has always backfired—the Christians increased!

China's leadership is clearly alarmed and nervous about the unexpected groundswell of what they call "religious fever" in their Marxist society for still another reason. The people-revolutions in the European countries made China's Communist leaders suspicious that the religious convictions of Europe's people were somehow behind the overthrow of their Marxist governments. They don't want the same thing to happen in China, hence the renewed crackdown on Christians.

The wonderful flip side!

Revival amid repression is the way God's hand moves. Along with growing persecution, Christians in China are once more experiencing revival. A strong move of God is sweeping across Anhui, Henan, Sichuan, Fujian, Guangdong, and Zhejiang provinces with thousands coming to Christ daily in a religious awakening led mostly by young people and students. As government restrictions on Christian worship increased in flood-ravaged Anhui province, whole villages reportedly were turning to Christ. Christians in more prosperous provinces such as Zhejiang, south of Shanghai, are providing money to build church buildings. As prosperous farmers, they have greater freedom. Church building goes on almost unhindered in remote regions, even in Yunnan and Inner Mongolia.

Believers are aware that martyrdom is possible for some Christian leaders and many grass-roots Christians, even as Communism lies on its death bed. But they have counted the cost before and go full speed ahead with their witness. O

10

Survivors Of A
Hundred Storms

To better understand China and the Chinese people whom we may encounter either in our own country or in our travels or work in China, let us take a closer look at different segments of China's society. We will do that in the next few chapters starting from the top to the bottom—the top being China's oldest citizens. Let us note that the Marxist hard line political leaders of China today are in this elder category. We will invest more space in describing the lifestyles of the elderly because they are interwoven with the rest of the generational categories. We gain insights into what other age groups are going through and what China's people have been struggling for.

China has undergone extraordinary changes within the lifetime of the present elderly—they are without question "survivors of a hundred storms." Many began life during a dynastic regime rooted in thousands of years. They lived through the upheavals that established a fledgling republic in 1911. A heavy-handed Communist dictator grabbed the reins of state in 1949 and turned China upside down for an entire generation. Within the last decade modernization struggled to the forefront with economic reforms, but political control was still clenched in the aging but iron grip of China's Marxist leaders.

Bloody civil wars, the tragic military rape and occupation of China by Japan, revolutions, gyrating class struggle, brainwashing, extermination of millions of Chinese, privation, and physical suffering constantly threatened their daily lives. The elderly painfully remember it all because they were among those jerked back and forth between polarized political philosophies. In a totalitarian state people must comply with whatever erratic or fanatical policies are current—or die.

China's present elderly have courageously weathered inconceivable political, economic, and social storms. Their fortunes and lifestyles rose and fell with the tide of China's ever-changing society and values.

Those now in their sixties were in their prime during the madness of the so-called "Cultural Revolution." Some of them were caught up in and went along with the political insanity. The educated and professionals were humiliated by Chairman Mao's rampaging teenage Red Guards and deprived of their academic positions. Some were sent to the countryside to labor with and "learn from" the peasants. Others were imprisoned for decades or killed. Private property was seized by the state, families were separated, schools closed, and a whole generation was robbed of educational opportunity.

Those who outlasted the atrocities tried to pick up the pieces after the revolution with characteristic Chinese resilience. Political rehabilitation gave some a short reprieve to pursue an education and try to make a belated contribution to society. They are now China's elderly. Some of their children are today's urban work force or the new class of farmers, professionals, and leaders. Some of their grown children and grandchildren are studying abroad; some of their precious grandchildren died in the '89 massacre of students peacefully demonstrating for democracy in Tiananmen Square.

People of the royal walking sticks

The whole world knows of China's strong tradition of respect for the elderly. In the third century B.C. ancient bamboo tablets record that the elderly came under protection of the law. The royal court presented to people over age 70 a specially designed cane with a carved turtledove on top. Anyone possessing it enjoyed special favors in society, social status on a par with officials, and exemption from taxes.

The punishment for anyone found guilty of mistreating or insulting the aged was to be beheaded! As far back as the 6th century B.C. the philosopher Confucius and later Mencius taught filial obedience not only to one's own parents but to the parents of others.

China's senior citizens no longer receive actual royal walking sticks, but hopefully, after a tumultuous lifetime, a new day may be dawning for their well-being, their continued happiness, and self-esteem. That is our prayer.

China has and will continue to have *the largest group of elderly people in the world!* According to the United Nations criterion which considers everyone over 60 in the aged category, *China now has 90 million senior citizens*—projected to reach 130 million in ten years. By comparison, the United States has approximately 27 million people over 65.

Although nearly half of the one billion plus population of China today are under 30, the number of China's elderly continues to climb by 1.8 million each year. Improved health care and living standards have extended life expectancy from about 35 years before 1949 to 68 in 1982. At the other end of the age scale, China is trying to check its astronomical population growth by legislating one child per family.

Pensions and retirement benefits

Who takes care of the elderly in their "evening years," as Chinese call the later years of life? What happens when they are no longer able to manage? Being part of a family with "three generations under one roof" is still considered by the elderly in China to be the ideal way to spend their later years. This tradition is reinforced by the official Marriage Code which stipulates that "children have the duty to support and assist their parents" and that "grandchildren who have the capacity to bear the relevant costs have the same duty toward their grandparents whose children are deceased." In both urban and rural communities it's common for elderly parents to live with one of their children, with the other siblings sharing in the expense.

How then will the compulsory one-child-per-family policy affect this? As these only children mature and marry, society will be moving toward still greater modernization. Social planners recognize that one adult child would potentially be responsible to support four grandparents and two parents. They will have no other siblings to share the burden of care and cost. The present trend of one-child families also means that the proportion of elderly will become greater in coming decades. Obviously, the government has had to institute alternate means of support for the elderly, especially for those without families and those not having pensions. Today the trend is toward an increase in society's role in providing for the security, health, and happiness of the aging.

The elderly grew up in the era when the government assigned every man and woman to do productive work from teen years on. The government, as "Big Brother," managed every facet of Chinese life from the cradle to the grave. During the "Cultural Revolution" even marriages had to have government approval and were based on political affinity. This broke the ancient yoke of marriage arrangements by parents. All of life and one's very identity were dictated by the appointed work place. The possibility of changing jobs or learning new skills during one's lifetime was remote.

The system had its social guarantees, however. You had a job from which you could not be fired. You were guaranteed a salary, but it was frozen and the same as everyone else's, not based on your skill or productivity. Your work place provided housing, medical needs, child care, and education. When you retired, you received a pension paid by the factory or work place. For lifetime state employees in urban areas, pensions range from 75 to 100 percent of one's previous salary and free medical service continues.

Help on a national scale

There will always be circumstances which keep many of the elderly from living with their families or independently. The urban elderly who live alone through choice or other reasons have special problems. Government publications would have us believe that the elderly are now being looked after adequately, but in reality many of China's senior citizens fall through the cracks and suffer great privation.

Great strides have been made, but China has a long way to go to achieve the utopia for the elderly that is painted so idealistically in her periodicals. According to official sources Beijing, to name one city, has organized 20,000 groups of volunteers, many of them young people, to visit the elderly regularly and help with shopping, haircuts, cleaning, and home repairs.

China reports that more than 30,000 "Homes for the Aged" in urban and rural areas have been established, something unheard of before. As nuclear families become more the norm in cities, the number of senior citizen apartment complexes is growing. Most of them are said to provide not only housing but meal service, medical care, and recreational facilities. Dietitians, specialists in diseases of the elderly, and exercise advisers are on call. China is concerned to maintain the ancient tradition of respect for the elderly as an integral part of socialist ethics.

More activities are being planned by the government for

China's elderly today. Work units and tea houses sponsor arts festivals for the aged. They gather in parks carrying pet birds in cages for a daily outing. Hanging the cages on tree branches, older gentlemen play cards or chess along the street. They attend Chinese operas and plays and gather to play traditional Chinese instruments. Magazines, newspapers, radio, and television are now featuring stories about the elderly. Books and magazines are newly published for them. A newspaper and a publishing house geared for the elderly are under preparation.

Some 200 colleges or correspondence institutes cater to the elderly. China has established over 70 "Schools for Elderly People" across the country and more are on the way. Such institutions were undreamed of a generation ago because no one thought they were necessary. Subjects range from gardening, cooking, sports, and hobbies to history, calligraphy, painting, music, and literature.

China's seniors are said to be moving away from the previous dullness and monotony of their sunset years into the spirited and healthy frame of mind that comes from being optimistic participants in life. Hopefully this will foster a new warmth in their relationships with members of their families and neighbors, making them less domineering and demanding of their children. China has come far in her renewed concern for her elderly—but the road is long.

The rural elderly

Peasants and farmers comprise 80 percent of China's population. There the elderly have special problems in these changing times. Seventy million above age 60 live in the countryside without the pension system back-up of their urban counterparts. For thousands of years peasants labored in the fields as long as they were physically able, then their own families readily cared for them. In the countryside, "social security" under the Communist system takes the form of the "five guarantees"—food, clothing, fuel, basic education of their children, and burial expenses. This system is administered at the production team level for the benefit of those who do not have the ability to earn a living. That includes the elderly.

No longer are all rural families in a position to care for their own elderly. Since the commune system was scrapped, villages are becoming more prosperous as collectives. They are trying to cope by building modest retirement complexes for the childless elderly, the widowed, and those who have outlived their immediate families, or have no other means of care.

Traditionally, funerals in China were lavish and costly affairs. Under the Communist government they have become much simpler, consisting of a ceremony for paying last respects to the deceased, or a memorial gathering. Cremation is commonly practiced in the cities because of lack of cemetery space. Most Chinese still strongly oppose it out of traditional reverence for ancestors. Nevertheless, the all-controlling government demands it. Burial is more customary in the countryside, though coffins are buried deeper than in the West in order to conserve farmland. In China, white is the traditional color of mourning, but today in cities black arm bands are worn by family members of the deceased.

Not a high cholesterol crowd!

China's elderly are generally remarkably healthy without concern for cholesterol. Their diet doesn't contain much meat or fat or sugar. A scarcity of rich food and money to buy it has forced most of the population to a frugal but basically healthy daily diet of vegetables, rice, fish, very little meat and oil, and some fruit. A blessing in disguise! Exotic Chinese cuisine is, of course, world famous, but it is not common fare for ordinary folks in China.

Most of the elderly are active physically. The bicycle is still China's basic means of transportation—not for sport or exercise. China's elderly keep bicycling as they did from childhood. Each morning the parks and streets of China are crowded with the exercising elderly. *Taijiquan* (slow shadow boxing in prescribed movements) or other traditional martial arts exercises are especially popular. Would you believe a new fad is "disco dancing" for the elderly—and classic exercises are sometimes performed to "rock" music? In a Communist society!

Jogging for exercise is not as common as running. An "Old People's Long March Long-Distance Running Team" has been organized in Beijing with more than 800 members. Three Chinese oldsters were among the 10 runners who finished first among 1,000 elderly from 19 countries racing at the foot of Mt. Fuji in Japan. Cross-city races for the elderly in Beijing are popular—women participate as well.

Keep moving. . .

Of course, many retirees in China are happy to sit in the sun like their American counterparts in Florida, chat with their friends, or care for their grandchildren. But China recognizes that when these seniors were younger, many contributed significantly to building New China. The government encourages those who have special skills and talents to continue to use them even though they have been required to give younger people a chance by accepting early retirement. Millions of retirees who are in good health volunteer to serve in some kind of part-time paid or voluntary positions. This enhances their self-esteem and benefits society.

As advisors or consultants, many continue to exercise valuable abilities developed over a lifetime. Some 40 percent of retirees in China engage in some useful work. Retired teachers offer classes to help young teachers raise their professional level. Some are instructors in business, cooking, tailoring, music, painting, ancient crafts, and other technical or artistic skills.

Their services are probably appreciated most in their own communities: serving on neighborhood committees, mediating family disputes, (a common practice accepted and welcomed in China) heading neighborhood crime-prevention groups, and looking after people's homes, property, and children. China's citizens are accustomed to seeing retirees at busy intersections with their identifying volunteer arm bands helping to keep public order and direct pedestrian traffic.

Not good to be alone

Chinese tradition regarded the remarriage of widows and widowers as something of an insult to their families. Although China's official Marriage Law protects the right of widows to remarry, old ideas die hard. Some young people oppose their parent's remarriage for fear of "losing face" (public disgrace). Others are afraid of losing part of their inheritance to a step-parent or having to find another place to live if they've been living with parents because of housing shortages.

Nevertheless, many elderly widows and widowers in China are braving the deep-seated feudal tradition, overcoming their own inhibitions, and remarrying. Neighborhood committees and former work places often act as informal matchmakers for people who have lost spouses. Some cities even have matchmaking agencies to help provide introductions for the elderly—a sign that China has truly entered a new era!

China's seasoned saints

But we are keenly concerned whether there are Christians among China's enormous number of elderly. Our inquiry is tied to the question, *did any Christians survive in China?* After China's devastating "Cultural Revolution" (1966-1976), China's government led the outside world to believe that religion had been eradicated.

Two generations came on the scene in China without any contact with Christianity as brought from the outside world. Only China's grandparent generation could possibly have remembered the foreign missionary era. Young Christians, or any believers born after the late 1940s, wouldn't even know about the foreign missionary enterprise in China.

We have seen that in the late 1970s, after more than thirty years of isolation, China resumed diplomatic relations with the outside world. Early visitors hardly expected to find vestiges of the church. *Surprised by joy,* they found that Christianity not only survived the political inferno with its bloodshed, purges, and chaos, but *faith in Jesus Christ had multiplied* in what many call the greatest example of church growth since the early church!

How could such a miracle have happened? True faith in Jesus continued to burn in the hearts of Chinese believers. *The fruit of missions remained.* In the New Testament model, faithful Chinese Christians gathered their families, at the risk of their lives, to worship in the secrecy of their own homes. They not only kept their personal faith alive, but reproduced it by nurturing their children in the faith and witnessing to relatives and trusted friends. We call these gatherings "house churches" in New Testament terminology.

One of the significant factors in the survival and growth of personal Christian faith in China was the faithful broadcast of the gospel from outside transmitters by Christian ministries. Although listening to religious programs was illegal for many years at the height of the "Cultural Revolution," spiritually hungry people persisted in listening at the risk of their lives. Radio ministry was a wonderful and strategic way for Christians from the West and concerned Chinese Christian compatriots to touch China for Christ.

By one-to-one witness—neighbor to neighbor, factory worker to fellow laborer, farmer to farmer, student to student, doctor to patient—the gospel spread like wildfire throughout China. When Christians were thrown into prison, they counted it as God's opportunity to evangelize the other prisoners while suffering as Paul and Silas did. Details on the growth of the church in China are discussed in the chapter "The Church Triumphant."

The witness of the elderly

The elderly who were Christians during that period had and continue to have the greatest freedom to "gossip the gospel" everywhere—in villages, rural areas, big cities. They enjoy more mobility because they are no longer tied to a work place. Officials pay little attention to them. When pastors and men leaders were exiled to labor camps or imprisoned, God generously gave gifts by His Spirit to many women, especially the elderly, to preach and teach the Word and nurture new-born Christians.

Chinese Christians who were cast into prison in their prime, if they survived, became senior saints seasoned by suffering by the time they were released. Virtually all pastors and Christian workers in the churches that the Communist government allowed to open again after 1979 were the elderly who for decades had patiently endured suffering for the sake of Christ.

Elderly Christians were overjoyed to once again be permitted to publicly gather for worship without fear for their lives. Newly opened churches were packed with seasoned saints and newborns with whom they had shared the gospel in the dark years.

The leadership of the house churches likewise depended upon elderly Christians. With Bible schools and seminaries in China closed for over 30 years, no new leadership had been formally trained.

Hundreds of thousands of youth, educated in atheism and now disillusioned with Communism, are seeking meaning in life and turning to Christ. They swell the crowds in both the registered churches and house churches. These youthful inquirers need someone to teach them about God, point them to His Word, and disciple their early steps in Christ. Elderly pastors exclaim, "Formerly, shepherds looked for sheep—now sheep are looking for shepherds!" Today's church in China is in a leadership crisis that elderly Christians are still faithfully trying to alleviate.

Seizing opportunities

We have seen that because of mandatory early retirement many elderly live with their adult children, help with marketing and household tasks, and care for grandchildren while both parents work. During working hours the elderly are highly visible in parks, on the streets, and in market areas pushing strollers or with toddlers in tow. Seizing the spiritual opportunity, elderly Christians eagerly influence their grandchildren for Christ in an atheistic culture. They witness as well to their peers whom they encounter daily in their neighborhood, on the street, and in the tea house.

Elderly Christians in rural areas have far more freedom to spread the gospel than those in cities because government agencies find it nearly impossible to control religious activities in the countryside. The majority of China's millions of believers gather in rural house churches, in open courtyards, or in simple structures for worship which they build themselves. Elderly Christians with the fire of the Holy Spirit in their hearts continue to lead these flourishing groups.

Both the young and the elderly carry on itinerant evangelism, traveling constantly and at personal risk to teach the Word, encourage believers, and distribute Scriptures the length and breadth of China. Such religious activity is against the policy of the government but China's Christians obey God rather than man. At this writing, many of the newly imprisoned for their faith are the elderly who persist in spreading the gospel. One imprisoned Christian brother in his seventies testified, "I only pray for the release of my fellow prisoners, not for myself. As long as I stay in prison, I have a chance to lead to Christ those who would otherwise never hear the gospel." O

11

The Original "Lost Generation"

Let's look next at today's PARENT generation in China—the adult children of the senior citizens we discussed in the last chapter. They are approximately in their late thirties to late forties, somewhat counterparts to our "baby boomer" generation. Many of the scholars and researchers who have gone to study abroad are included in this group. If we want to cultivate friendships with them, it is helpful to understand what their growing years were like.

Many of them were "Red Guards," the rampaging teens turned loose by Mao when he attempted to fan a fresh flame of revolutionary fervor in a generation that was born after the sacrifices and hard times of the early revolution. He planned to give them a taste of patriotism mixed with violence and "save" them for Communism. In the process he "wasted" them—the youngsters went wild and even out of his control. Mao's plan pitifully and tragically boomeranged.

Those teens were part of the over 250 million children born in China during the 1950s and '60s. As of this writing, they are the transition generation of young parents and those pushing middle age. They are the parents of today's youth who are getting turned on to Western ways. They are backing off still further than their parents from any Communist political involvement. That may be part of the reason why the parents of today's teens are allowing their youngsters more freedom and not clamping down on their sometimes outlandish behavior.

They remember their own feelings as teens when China was in the throes of the "Cultural Revolution." Today's parents are the ones whose education was severely disrupted. They were told by their leaders

90

that education was useless, that all culture was either feudalistic, capitalist, or revisionist. They had not only been given permission but a big push by their hero-leader, Mao, to *rebel against everything.*

After the death of Mao, the fall of the "gang of four," and the sudden change of direction toward achieving the Four Modernizations and catching up with the outside world, these young adults had to readjust their entire belief system. A substantial number felt deceived and used during the years of turmoil, and lost all interest in politics and collective efforts. Feelings of anarchy persisted, expressed in undisciplined habits. They lacked education and skills and found it hard to cope with the menial jobs to which they were assigned by the government. Some of those who had to wait for job assignments turned to drinking, gambling, and crime. Others began to study hard and try to develop new skills, but they were motivated mainly with the idea of making money for themselves, not with the desire to serve the state or improve society. They cynically considered such idealism as empty talk. They were bitter that the government they had trusted had been unjust in its dealings with them.

Of course, no generalization can fit all of the hundreds of millions of Chinese youth at that time, or the parents they have become now. Not only must individual differences and backgrounds be considered, but at any point there must be a three-way split even to describe characteristics: college students, urban workers, and rural youth all had particular distinctives and preoccupations. But by virtue of having spent their youthful years in China, certain values and ideas unite them.

Trying some new goals

In an effort to offset negative attitudes among the millions of young adults who would be the foundation of China's society for the next generation, the government tried new measures to bring them back into the Party fold. It offered new goals and ideas about state policies in agriculture and industry, re-instituted competitive exams for university entrance, and offered more opportunities for self-study and employment. Life goes on, adulthood is achieved, family responsibilities are assumed, therefore many went along and settled down to the new direction of society. What alternative was there? Many of our own "Woodstock" generation of the '60s have similarly adopted the nine-to-five suburban lifestyle.

91

This generation of parents who tried to pick up their education again were by then much older than average students. Having spent years in forced labor in the countryside or in factories, some were motivated to study again. They anticipated that China would need educated people and would restore the status of intellectuals. This newly educated class had wide interests, began to think independently, and expressed keen curiosity about Western philosophy and political systems.

They were no longer satisfied with political slogans. They became ardent advocates of reform although they recognized that China is still a poor country, bureaucracy is an on-going problem, and feudal ways of thinking and behaving remain strong. They wrestled with a major question: Is a Western democratic system or a Marxist-based policy more realistic for China at this stage? They often walked on the fence, but as the years went by, jumped off more frequently on the free enterprise side.

Early hopes dashed

Most of this group hoped for high-level, lifelong job security because of their education. Their goals were simple: get a good job, earn lots of money, marry, and set up a comfortable home. Some still added "make the country strong and prosperous while attaining personal happiness." A small portion of this group realized their dream of being sent abroad for advanced study and research.

Such was the background of some of the parents of today's teens. Their expectations that the educated, the teachers, the intellectuals in Chinese society would certainly enjoy high status and high pay have been dashed, as we shall see. In her obsession for modernization, China should certainly have valued this strategic newly-educated class, and seen to it that they were rewarded and further motivated by at least an adequate salary system. Instead, teachers are near the bottom of the pay scale in China today; few want to enter the profession, and teachers are leaving their schools in droves for the business world. We shall discuss this more thoroughly in the chapter "Chaos in the Classroom."

In the days of revolutionary madness, China literally killed off her intellectuals. In her present days of materialistic madness, China is again, more subtly but just as surely, killing off her intellectuals.

The urban "lost generation"

A majority of the work force in China's factories, industries, mines, and city enterprises are the former teens who lived through or were part of the "Cultural Revolution." They are included in today's parent generation. Those who came back from the countryside and didn't pursue their education were assigned by the government to factories where they were greeted with anything but enthusiasm. These were formerly revolutionary hot-heads, now cooled by years of countryside labor. They arrived with "no basic skills, empty heads, and bad attitudes," according to a background story on youth in *China Reconstructs*, October 1983.

As soon as many of them started earning regular wages, they spent them on fancy clothes, hairstyles, and whatever new consumer goods appeared in the stores. They had little interest in work, were lazy and cocky, and confident that the Communist-socialist system guaranteed that they could not be fired. Factories, industries, and schools provided housing for their employees and families in a common location, meager though it was. The government froze salaries and there were no opportunities to get ahead. So why work hard?

This was indeed typical in the early years, but it was eventually replaced by the "responsibility system." No longer could workers depend on their "iron rice bowl" (holding a job permanently regardless of performance). Compensation and rewards became linked to individual effort. Now they had a chance to improve their incomes and win promotions if production could be boosted in their unit or factory. The government made major efforts to raise the educational level of those already employed through part-time and short-term courses, correspondence and TV schools, and self-study advisory services. Many of the current parent generation have done quite well.

What parents think of parenting

A Chinese maxim declares that the worst manifestation of disrespect for one's parents is not having children. Today there is an anguishing political twist that not only encourages but legislates parents either to have no children or to limit a couple to only one. Traditional Chinese culture has always placed great importance on raising children and this is underscored today when, so to speak, all the eggs are in one basket.

A survey among parents in China reported in *Beijing Review*, February 1989 that 86.5 percent stated that parents should have children, 11.5 percent that it isn't important to have children, and only 1.9 percent felt that it is better not to have children.

More men selected the statement "one should have children," whereas more women opted for the second and third responses. This reflects the rising economic and social status of women in China today and their felt need to achieve success in their careers and express their individuality—a new, un-traditional phenomenon in China.

The under-thirty generation and students tended not to put as great importance on having children as did older respondents. Those with a higher level of education were also less likely to place importance on children. Success in their own careers apparently took priority. Individual laborers and retired people considered children important.

When questioned about motivation to have children, traditional Chinese concepts of continuing the family line and children being necessary to support their parents in later life were low on the scale. This probably reflects the greatly improved social conditions and comparatively secure, comfortable lifestyles. Almost half of the respondents answered that it was one's duty to bring up children, and another third stated "without children, one's life is not satisfying."

We have seen in the previous chapter that children used to be viewed as a roof and meal ticket for aging parents who required the care of their grown children. In socialist China, guaranteed pensions for retirees and government-assumed responsibility for their basic needs have replaced the urgency of care by their children. Many parents still feel strongly that male children are considered preferable, but it isn't the critical issue that it was in centuries past. The idea that it was necessary to raise a family has changed from an extremely materialistic and pragmatic view of having children to doing what brings personal happiness. O

12

Chaos In The Classroom

The occupation of TEACHING is closely related to the PARENT generation. This age group normally produces teachers and professors for the educational system. The quantity and quality of teachers determines the direction of the next generation in any country. How has it gone in China?

Looking back over our shoulders

For thousands of years, in China's social hierarchy the scholar was most highly esteemed. China's examination system for imperial service remained almost unchanged for centuries, designed to select the most intelligent and promising young people to serve the government. Theoretically, the son of any Chinese family could take the exams. But because it required many years of private tutoring in the classics, (no public education was available) and facility in China's complicated language, few workers' and peasants' sons ever made the grade. Females, even from wealthy families, were ineligible. Learning was a status symbol providing life enrichment, not necessarily pursued for financial gain.

Along came the Communist government dedicated to achieving what it called the "dictatorship of the proletariat." Because 80 percent of China's people live in rural areas, Chairman Mao, the great helmsman of change, attempted to destroy the traditions and classic old system. He elevated "the masses." The new ideal esteemed the laborer above the intellectual. Workers, peasants, and soldiers were at the top of the status scale. They must be educated too, but in the Communist curriculum: basic Chinese language, arithmetic, elementary science, physical education, but above all, *political studies*. Usually the latter completely overshadowed the rest.

It is important to understand what is meant by the term "intellectual" as used in China. In *Beijing Review,* July 23-29, 1990, in an article "Intellectuals Contribute to Modernization," the writer explains,

> In China, the term "intellectuals" refers to people with a secondary or higher educational level as well as those who have a higher technical title than assistant engineer. In 1989, there were 22.18 million intellectuals in China, one-third of whom had received a college education.

Manual labor top priority

It was a peasant revolution that brought victory to the Red Army and helped establish the Communist government. Therefore agricultural priorities were critical to China's success and prosperity. Mao decided to reverse the policy of Mencius, one of China's great philosophers, who declared, "He who works with his head rules; he who works with his hands is ruled." Mao declared that work was more noble. It was to be an integral part of the lives of young people at school and at home.

He turned social customs upside down by declaring that men should not be ashamed to help with household chores at home (unheard of in traditional China) and sent all women off to work too. That doubled his work force. Writers, artists, musicians, and teachers shouldn't be afraid to roughen their hands by digging or plowing. He implemented that policy to the extreme at the height of the revolution by putting teachers, musicians, and all "white collar" intellectuals into factories, labor camps, and out in the countryside to work under the authority of illiterate farmers. In the process, he literally buried the prime of China's future creative leadership in the grave of stupidity.

"Serving the people" through manual labor became the overworked slogan from nursery schools through university. Primary school children were put to work repairing and cleaning their schools and keeping public parks and streets tidy. College students had to do the same, building their own facilities, and going to the factory or countryside during vacation to "learn from the peasants." Mao began work-study programs to integrate theoretical and practical work throughout the curriculum for both students and teachers—all designed to bring scholars out of the ivory tower.

But the negative political and social changes which resulted from the extremes of such policies completely undermined that tower. The whole structure crumbled in a way the leaders didn't anticipate. After the death of Mao, certain leaders even within the Communist party recognized the pitiful state of their country and moved toward reform, revisionism, some free enterprise, and a modified capitalism. They knew they'd have to change the picture or China would be down the drain. China not only opened to the outside world but took a deep breath and determined to catch up with it. When China's floodgates opened, we have seen that Western values and ways came in like a torrent.

Education back to square one

It seemed that finally education was again coming into its own. The remnants of the intellectuals who survived the humiliation and rigors of peasant life, labor camps, or prisons were reinstated after having lost the very best years of their lives through revolutionary madness policies forced upon them. Schools at every level had actually been closed during the "Cultural Revolution" when Red Guards ravaged the land with the blessing of Mao—especially targeting the educated. Now the government reopened the schools and gave young people the opportunity for an education of sorts. Learning was again in favor, and considered essential for the country and for personal advancement, but not necessarily for life enrichment, as under the classic system.

Then the swinging pendulum again. Revolutionary political thought and feelings gradually faded when China began to open to the outside world. Personal financial gain became the prime mover, and the government was thought of only as the vehicle that would either allow or hinder the speed of increasing one's own bank account. "Serve the people" was no longer a slogan on the lips of ordinary people. More often it was "Serve yourself and your family."

At this writing, another swing of the pendulum: teacher and student dropouts are escalating alarmingly in China at every level, while work and business enjoy new prestige. The youth, especially, are looking around and deciding that they don't need an education—a dangerous mindset.

Who wants to be a teacher?

The inevitable result is that the classic admiration of and respect for teachers, bordering on reverence, has experienced a tragic reversal. China's institutions of higher learning are already experiencing a shortage of instructors. About half of the country's 400,000 teachers in China's 1,075 universities and colleges are below age 40 and termed "young teachers." The current trend among these young teachers is to change to other occupations or go abroad, according to the *Guangming Daily*. These were the hope of China, the highly motivated ones who struggled to reverse their label as "the lost generation" by forging ahead with their educations against tremendous odds. They are among the parents of today's teens.

Why would they want to give up teaching? Shortage of housing for teachers, low pay, and slim chances for advancement contribute to their lack of interest to continue teaching. Beside waiting lists for housing, lecturers can't support themselves or a spouse and child on 97 yuan a month, or on 70 yuan as faculty assistants. Many professors still have to depend on their parents or relatives for financial help. Hopes for young university teachers to be promoted to full professorships are virtually impossible, according to *China Daily*. Teachers throughout China generally earn less than factory workers, bank employees, and technological personnel.

China Youth News reported in early 1989 that the number of high school graduates wanting to be teachers continues to drop. Even key Normal universities find it increasingly difficult to recruit students. The vice-president of a teachers university in Guangzhou said that students are "dragged in and forced out." The income gap between educators and business people is a compelling reason.

The *China Daily*, May 1989, admitted to alarmist talk by reporting that all of China is beginning to believe that it isn't profitable to study. This is in contrast to the "Cultural Revolution" years when schools were closed and students were *unable* to study, although they *wanted to*. Now they *may*, but *don't want to!* This is the case at all levels of education in China. The *China Daily* reported,

Between 1980 and 1988 more than 4 million primary and middle school students quit school. In 1988 alone more than 6,000 college students and 2,000 post-graduate students left school. Because teachers also resigned to get jobs that would pay a living wage, schools in some areas were forced to close. The alarm is already sounding when 35 percent of China's population above the age of 15 is illiterate or half-literate. The situation could affect social standards and threaten the survival of this nation.

The key to the teacher's desk

An article from the Beijing-based *Economic Weekly* attributed the dangerous situation to China's investment of only 3.7 percent of its gross national product in education. In a country with a tradition of appreciation for scholars it is like committing cultural suicide to neglect scholarship.

To restore itself to intellectual health, the article suggested that China should be giving double doses of educational encouragement to its young intellectuals and youth. But the education budget per person equals only one-fourth that of other developing countries. The auditing of education expenditures has also turned up the misuse of funds in the already meager budget.

The State should stop hosting feasts with public money, importing luxury cars, and constructing unnecessary extra official buildings, and start cracking down on tax evaders. Stopping big leaks could generate money to improve the living standards of teachers.

Most of the outside world doesn't realize that China's higher education system is free of charge and the government provides every student with accommodations and board right on the school premises without cost. That makes the current educational system incredibly costly and compounds the problem of low budget. No funds are left to pay teachers a living wage. Implementing a tuition fee, the article went on, and encouraging universities to admit more students at their own expense, and to offer financial assistance only to those who need it are constructive measures of reform.

One more startling suggestion: "Citizens and foreign investors should be encouraged to set up schools." That would be a flashback to pre-revolution days and certainly a major switch in China's socialist philosophy of self-sufficiency and non-interference by outsiders. Lastly, the article suggested, both rural and urban education should be made more practical and students trained to apply their knowledge to the real economic world. ○

13

Another "Lost Generation"?

Let's look in more detail at the condition of China's YOUTH today. These are the teenage and college age children of the parent generation we have described in the previous chapter, born after the "Cultural Revolution" or as it was winding down.

The parents of today's youth were the hopeless, cynical, rebellious, uneducated, and disillusioned ones who returned to the cities from the countryside. With typical Chinese resilience, they managed to survive and settle down like America's radical "flower children" of the seventies. They married and had their "one child per family" offspring, whom they spoiled with attention. The Chinese refer to such children as "little emperors." The first generation of "little emperors" are today's youth, now in their teens or mid-twenties, which is the average age in China. Those who may have married at an earlier age than their parents had been allowed to, are already raising the second generation of pampered, overprotected "little emperors." We'll meet them in the next chapter.

The older ones in urban areas may be in college or university. However, out of China's immense population only 1.9 million are undergraduate students, and only 97,000 are graduate students in colleges and universities. Only about 4 percent of middle school graduates gain admission to college. Other youth may be in their first factory jobs, roaming urban streets unemployed, trying to get started in little private enterprises, or joining gangs of delinquents to commit crimes. *Beijing Review* reported early in 1992 that young people under 25 years of age were now responsible for about 75 percent of all criminal cases. How is it in rural areas? Their "country cousins" may now be doing far better financially than their parents since at least limited private ownership of property and personal profit is permitted.

Afflicted with "study blahs"

According to China's own media, "our young people today are apathetic, self-centered, and concerned only with making money and getting ahead." The *Xinhua* newspaper in May 1989, just before the Tiananmen demonstrations, referred to China's youth as "another lost generation." But this time they were absent from the halls of learning voluntarily. The *Beijing Review* in their section on events and trends reported that "study blahs" are hitting students.

> Books and courses are no longer attractive. Academic boredom is becoming a common mindset among college and postgraduate students. . . .At Fudan University in Shanghai, between 8 and 10 a.m., only 40 percent of students were cracking the books. Of other students, 10 percent were chatting and 10 percent were watching movies on television. Seven percent were with their sweethearts, and the remaining 33 percent were otherwise [non-academically] occupied. All this points to the fact that knowledge is losing its glamour. Actually, this book-weariness started a few years ago when many students took a shine to the slogan: 'Long Live Mark 60.' (A grade of 60 is the minimum passing grade on an exam)

Where has all the thinking gone?

Among the reasons given for academic apathy among China's youth is that intellectuals, as we have seen, are generally not paid good salaries for their jobs. Many students are thinking, "A master's degree will bring in 82 yuan a month and a doctorate, 89. With skyrocketing prices, how can that pittance support us?" Students without higher education are making a bundle of money in business, some self-employed. "Educational malpractices" leave students yawning. Traditional ways of teaching are boring and the curriculum isn't relevant to current society or the students' interests. A colorful social life and any kind of amusement is a greater lure than study. The above article continued,

> Some students think that good marks prove nothing because almost all students cheat during exams. But making money is a true sign of success. The quest for money has become addictive. . . and the current trend is an omen to society, especially educational circles, that something is seriously amiss.

Over the past few years, all across China many market stalls appeared right on university campuses run by students eager to earn money. *China Youth News* claims that students involved are disrupting academic pursuit. On the other hand, some people have praised this blossoming entrepreneurial spirit. Students sell everything from groceries, cooked foods, books, and rock music cassette tapes to tee-shirts, blue jeans, sunglasses, and imported cigarettes.

The voices of youth

A recent survey asked 450 Beijing students what issues were important to them on campus. *Zhongguo Qingnian Bao* (China Youth News) in March 1989 reported these:

Middle school students were not sure they wanted to pursue further education because starting from 1993, the state would no longer secure jobs for college graduates. They would be on their own, sink or swim. Students want to work part-time during vacations to earn pocket money, but casual jobs are hard to find. The students want the right to choose their own teachers. An increasing number of students falling in love at an early age has become a new problem of much social concern. Students are uneasy about the growing practice of charging each other money for help in doing homework. Many students want to introduce individual competition into the classroom to take the place of the Communist-socialist tradition of "the group goes forward together."

The issues continued: Smoking by even young students is far out of control. Students complain that they have no place to go for after-school refreshment and activities. They resist the practice of some schools to collect money from students under all sorts of pretexts. Students lack a sense of security. Some lawbreakers publicly extort money from students or take liberties with women students right in front of school gates.

The attitude of youth in China today seems to be "live for today, make money, imitate the West, and have a good time." They are trying to feed on husks that will never fill the emptiness that materialism and consumerism only creates.

Who dropped the reins?

Why is the Communist government apparently looking the other way and allowing the youth in China to parrot the West? We may venture a guess that the Communist government in part tolerated the new laxity in order to win over China's youth to other policies of the government.

Possibly the leaders intended to allow only a limited amount of private enterprise, just enough to appease the growing restlessness of the people and bring them back in line to Communist loyalties. But having smelled the roast, and tasted a bite, the people, especially the youth, want to gobble the whole pig. The policy opened the proverbial "Pandora's Box" and the government seems unable to control the wild spirit of capitalism.

Because today's youth don't have the same revolutionary incentive as their parents, naturally they care little about Marxist idealism. They have no incentive to help create a classless society or to serve the masses. Their concerns seem to have become almost totally mercenary. Young people want to find the quickest way to "make a buck," or lots of bucks, and intend to spend their money immediately on the newly available consumer goods.

After all, only China's grandparent generation remembers the days of Russian influence. The younger generation was never involved in spewing hatred and shouting slogans against the American imperialists. They grew up during the thawing of icy relations with the United States. So they naturally crave and lust after everything Western or American to the grief of the old guard in the Marxist government. To China's youth, capitalism is far from a dirty word—it is gilded with gold.

Memories are short or non-existent

How many in China remember the revolutionary "Long March" that launched the Communist revolution? Only the conservative Marxist old guard in their late seventies and eighties who are trying to hang on to the steering wheel of the careening Communist Party in China with shaking hands. The youth don't remember.

Who remembers the atrocities, rapes, and ravages by the Japanese during the thirties and forties? Only China's grandparent generation. The youth don't remember. Now they see China happily doing business with smiling, Western-suited Japanese. They only notice that there are more Japanese than any other group among the nearly 2 million foreign tourists climbing the Great Wall, roaming around the Forbidden City, and generously spending their yen.

Who remembers the "Cultural Revolution," a holocaust that makes the one in Europe seem like child's play. Deaths in China from revolution-related causes, wanton killings, and famine may have totaled 30 million people. That's nearly double the battlefield losses of all countries in World War II, *plus* the slaughter of Jews in Germany, *including* the massive Soviet purges and Stalin's terror. China's youth don't remember.

Of course it is hard to remember what you never experienced, or what the schools haven't taught in history classes. A letter was sent from a 15 year old Beijing middle school girl to the editor of *China Daily* a few months before the Tiananmen massacre. She wrote,

> When the 'Cultural Revolution' was going on, I was too small to remember anything. But when I see some pictures about the 'Revolution' on television, I feel eager to know what China was like at that time. I don't understand why millions of youths were raising a little red book and shouting slogans, many even with tears in their eyes. I don't understand why young people my age were so excited at torturing those grey beards at big rallies.

A parent wrote to the same newspaper,

107

How strange it is! After such a short time, the 'Cultural Revolution,' an unprecedented catastrophe for our nation, already has become something completely unknown to our children. Recalling my own experience as a 'Red Guard' in those years, I can't say that today's Chinese youths at some time in the future will not be crazily pouring into the streets again, incited by a 'revolutionary' slogan.* No one tells them what the 'Cultural Revolution' was really like, and no one has ever done any earnest and profound study on how that national disaster was launched and what the deep social reasons were. This is very dangerous.

* A few months after the above letter was published, it *was* happening! China's youth again took to the streets, but this time they were shouting "democracy" as the slogan. ○

14

Reign of
"Little Emperors"

Most of China's children seem to be well-dressed, healthy, bright-eyed, active, many clutching expensive toys—at least the ones that the tourist sees. The students and scholars from China with whom we make friends in our country have often left families behind that include young children (perhaps a single child, conforming to the one-child-per-couple government policy.)

There are 300 million children in China—equal to the whole population of North America! Officials warn that at least 24 million babies will be born in China in 1992 when a fertility peak will be magnified by the Chinese desire to bear children during the auspicious Year of the Monkey. In the *South China Morning Post*, December 1, 1991, the State Family Planning Commission chief reported that coupled with the slowing mortality, the surge in births will add at least 16 million to a population that will surpass 1.16 billion in 1992. The number of women in or entering the peak childbearing ages of 20-29 would soar by 1993 to a record 123.7 million. China's youthful population will be part of the startling projection that by the year 2000, nearly 50 percent of all people in Asia will be under 16 years of age!

What are today's children of China like? Zhang Huanhua, schoolmaster of a primary school in Beijing, observed:

> Children are too pampered since one couple is supposed to have only one child. Fearing that their children might suffer hardships, parents try to do everything for them. As a result, children become more and more self-centered. Instead of being considerate of

others, they take it for granted that they should be taken care of by others. These children grow up without the give and take of sibling rivalry or companionship. Their whole world revolves around themselves.

No wonder China's descriptive term for these spoiled children is "little emperors." The *South China Morning Post* reported in mid-1992 that the only child in China does not seem to struggle with the low self-esteem that often plagues young people in the West. That positive factor nevertheless produces the negative of selfishness and arrogance. And there is a new problem on the horizon for many of China's pampered children:

> Due to economic reforms which continue to raise living standards, Chinese children today will probably turn out to be the best educated and most self-confident generation in Chinese history. But prosperity is also proving to have at least one drawback for these children: *an unprecedented amount of obesity!*

Honor thy children?

It seems strange to see parents in China standing in buses while their spoiled children sit. You notice them waiting outside school gates to bring hot foods for their children, carrying their books home, and bowing to their every whim. Parents are quick to indulge them with expensive toys, video games, and hard to obtain foods sometimes at sacrifice to themselves.

According to China's media, courtesy, generosity, kindness, unselfishness, and thoughtfulness are not being instilled in China's children. A senior educator observed in *China Daily*, April 1989:

> Parents do not realize that over-indulging their children causes the children to take unlimited affection from their parents for granted and not do anything for them in return. Consequently, children become selfish in response to their parents' unselfish love. One whole generation was almost ruined in the 10-year chaotic "Cultural Revolution" when beating, looting and smash-

ing were rampant by youth and children. We should be careful not to plant similar seeds in our younger generation.

Spoiling them is nevertheless planting dangerous seeds of insensitivity and violence. The human heart is already bent toward evil, and it doesn't require much to push it over the edge. Hospital officials in China report that it is quite common for parents to be brought in who are victims of beatings by their children!

A survey revealed that only half of the surveyed children take care of their parents when they become ill. Screaming and kicking at their elders, parents, and grandparents, and showing disrespect are not rare. Unheard of in old China! In Shanghai, a child stabbed his father with a kitchen knife. When the police asked him whether he felt guilty about hurting his father, he replied, "How dare he try to scold me!"

Over-compensation

Parents in China today seem over-eager to see their children have what they didn't have and to make a name for themselves. They push their children to learn music, dance, painting, foreign languages, and other skills in spare time whether or not the children have interest or talent. Taking expensive lessons is a status symbol for children—but more often for parents. Charging for these lessons, low-paid school teachers can moonlight and earn a welcome second pay check. Behind this exaggerated drive for extra education is the fact that many parents who were once ambitious to establish themselves have given up hope to fulfill their own goals. Now they concentrate on pushing their one child full speed ahead.

Educational drop outs

At the same time, an alarming number of children are dropping out of school because they are getting the idea from society that it doesn't pay to get an education. Each year, according to the *Economic Daily*, May 1989, about 15 million *primary and middle school students* quit school.

In rural areas, uneducated parents don't relate to science and general knowledge and so don't encourage their children to stay in school. Moreover, schools are generally not well run. A 1986 report shows that 76.6 percent of all middle school teachers are unqualified. Classrooms are overcrowded and teaching facilities and equipment are poor.

In some areas of the Northwest, the government imposes heavy fines on parents to ensure that all children receive their full nine years of compulsory education. The fines are between 30 and 60 yuan in rural areas for each year of schooling a child misses. In cities the fines are heavier. Because some parents deliberately withdraw their children from school so they could work and increase the family income, fines of up to 5,000 yuan are imposed on firms that employ child labor.

China's children are quickly becoming the teenagers and young adults who will determine their country's future. Let us remember that China's children study in classrooms where atheism and evolution have been taught for several generations. The altruism of serving their country is not emphasized to the extent that it was when their parents were in school and Marxist studies prevailed. They are not provided with any moral absolutes. Schools are turning out self-serving persons who will be China's secular humanists.

If China's children also neglect their basic educational foundation, take up only materialistic values, and grow up without the traditional respect for their elders, China's direction is shaky. And without the knowledge of the gospel to transform them from within into loving, caring adults, they are in danger of becoming a *third* "lost generation."

Are we honest enough to examine our educational system in the United States and other Western countries on the foregoing points? Do we find it embarrassing to point an accusing finger at China? O

15

Planters Of Good Seed

To understand the current attitude of the Chinese government toward religion, and to help us share our faith with those in modern China, it is important to study the history of Christianity in China. The interpretation of certain events is sensitive and sometimes controversial even today. Our viewpoints tend to be clouded by nationalistic and cultural overtones on both the Chinese and the Western sides. In attempting to cover complex historical events in a very short space, I can only touch weighty issues briefly. Some of the information in this chapter overlaps material already covered, but in the context of missions, we are searching for insights on how certain events affected the spread of the gospel. *The Back of the Book* section includes resources which give more background on the subject.

Christianity is considered by China as another foreign religion because it came from outside the country. How it came, and in what company it came, turned out to be somewhat of a problem then and now.

The nature of the Great Commission crosses all national, political, social, and religious lines. However, barriers will always be there and must be dealt with. Regardless of the political resistance of a nation's government, for instance, its people need the saving message of the gospel. If we waited for a polite invitation from any secular, atheistic, or other-religion-dominated government, God's Good News would never penetrate a country. Christians carrying the gospel attempt to go where they believe God is sending them.

In previous chapters we have seen how China resisted foreign influences and how history verifies that foreign countries took advantage of China, inflicting disgraces and national humiliation upon her. Early missionaries to China were subjects and citizens of some of those countries. But it is unfair to imply that they were party to these imperialist activities, or that they approved of them. It is documented that British missionaries were very opposed to the terrible opium trade, deeply disturbed, and active in England with groups that were striving to stop it. Perhaps reluctantly, yet thankfully for the sake of the gospel, missionaries gained from the spin off of preferential treatment won for foreigners through the Unequal Treaties.

Missionaries from whatever country should not be held responsible for policies or activities of their governments, though they frequently suffer from the fallout. There are both evil and good influences in all governments, yet Christians are obliged to serve God within their own nation's framework. God may use our citizenship, as in the case of Paul, the Roman citizen. Or He may choose to bypass it. Historical examples abound. Even when evil seems to be triumphing, *God is sovereign.* We can see this in China from the beginnings of gospel penetration to the present, regardless of the vicissitudes of the political scene and China's complicated dealings with the outside world. Like the prophet Daniel, we should clearly see that God is in control of history, and in the end the Kingdom will be given to the "saints of the Most High."

In the same boat

Space does not permit dealing with several earlier attempts to establish Christianity in China: the Nestorians from the Middle East (653-845), and the Catholic efforts—the Franciscans (1280-1353) and the Jesuits (1542-1842). Suffice to say that by 1800, baptized Chinese Roman Catholic converts were said to number about 200,000. Protestant efforts are usually dated from the arrival of Robert Morrison of the London Missionary Society in 1807.

Foreign missionaries began coming to China in increasing numbers from 1860, after China lost the Second Opium War. They came riding up her rivers, sometimes literally on the gunboats of Western powers, possibly the only safe transportation available. That made the Chinese understandably suspicious. Unfortunately, from the beginning the gospel was somewhat entangled with Western exploitation, but only by association, not by intention.

In some cases when religious foreigners suffered injury, sometimes a few demanded reparations, but the majority were willing to suffer wrong for the gospel's sake. Because of China's war defeats missionaries were permitted to preach wherever they wished throughout the land without obtaining permission from controlling Chinese officials. *Only a few missionaries*, to be sure, used their political influence and privileged status to contravene Chinese law and protect some of their converts who got into trouble for various reasons. But it is also true that the questionable actions of a few tend to be remembered.

Because of harsh and unfamiliar living conditions in China, it would be expected that missionaries would need to bring with them some of the conveniences and amenities of their Western homelands. Sometimes they lived behind high mission compound walls. Because most of them worked among the poor and in rural areas, their standard of living naturally contrasted with that of those whom they sought to evangelize. The Chinese culture in which they felt God called them to serve was strange to them. They did not have the benefit of today's extensive seminary courses in cross-cultural living and witness, and Chinese civilization, culture, and history. They found it difficult to sort out what aspects of Chinese culture were to be appreciated and what were to be opposed. Of course some poor judgments were made and lessons were learned from those blunders by the missionaries who came later.

Identification with the Chinese people in that earlier century was difficult due to the vast contrast with their homeland living conditions. With genuine respect, we must recognize that a many missionaries spent a large part of their time in arduous travel, lived in Chinese inns and villages, often under very primitive conditions, and suffered illnesses for which no medical help was available. When they settled in a town, most of them lived in Chinese buildings and identified as best they could with the local people.

As an example, Hudson Taylor, founder of the China Inland Mission, insisted that his missionaries wear Chinese clothing. He pointed out that one of the main hindrances to the spread of the gospel was the "foreignness" evident in the attire and living quarters of missionaries in the large cities. Not all mission agencies agreed with his convictions. Opinions differed even among his own missionaries.

Without question, it was with good intentions that missionaries embarked upon the most extensive social ministries endeavors in the history of missions. Schools, free clinics, hospitals, and orphanages mushroomed across China. Missionaries applied their Western get-up-and-go and their genuine Christian compassion to hundreds of specialized projects such as girls' education, mental institutions, drug treatment, publishing houses, literacy work, disaster relief, agricultural modernization, nutrition improvement, and lobbying for legal reform. Among the greatest of these was Western-style higher education, with eventually 16 such colleges and universities in China. The contribution to China of the medical and educational efforts of foreign missions is acknowledged even by the Chinese government. Indeed, those institutions helped to build the foundation of modern China. Many of China's leaders benefitted from education in mission schools.

On the other hand, as the missionary effort became more institutionalized, it seemed to be less evangelistic and local church related—with notable exceptions.

Let us build your church

To the Chinese, missionaries appeared to have unlimited funds from the West at their disposal. Sometimes missionaries persisted in establishing Western style enterprises that seemed somewhat unnecessary or at least premature to the simple, fledgling Chinese church. But because the missionaries controlled the money and provided free leadership, Chinese Christians tended to offer little resistance. Of course the Chinese Christians benefitted from all of these religious institutions at the time, but it turned out that those Western institutions, traditions, and structures were maligned by the new Communist regime as imperialistic. Association with them caused much suffering for Chinese Christians when foreign missionaries were forced to leave China.

By all means, let us thank God for the positive side. In spite of shortcomings and misunderstandings, dedicated and sacrificial missionary efforts brought the simple gospel message of Christ's redeeming love and available salvation to China's millions. Preaching points were established in thousands of strategic places. Many grew into evangelistic chapels, usually under the leadership of Chinese Christian workers, who were sometimes employed by the missionaries. Some gradually became churches under missionary guidance, frequently with continued missionary leadership. As congregations became more spiritually mature, most missionaries made sincere attempts to turn the churches over to the Chinese congregations.

1926 was the peak year for missions in China. The Protestant missionary force reached 8,325 representing 157 mission societies, bolstered by some 13,500 Chinese workers ministering in about 12,000 churches and outstations. Altogether there were about 400,000 baptized Protestants and nearly 3,000,000 Catholic communicants. God had raised up numerous leaders of the faith in the Western world and sent these true pioneers to China. Spectacular breakthroughs and the sheer numbers of China's unevangelized seemed to justify the particular missionary approaches that were used at that time. China was looked upon as *the* mission field for all-out efforts by mission agencies and Western Christian churches.

Growing restlessness

But many Chinese felt uneasy. Christianity continued to be connected with "foreignness." Chinese converts often tended to put aside their Chinese culture and lifestyles to adopt foreign ways. During the recurring periods of war and political upheavals in China, foreign missionary work was at first cut back and then nearly abandoned. The still limited Christian education system had failed to provide enough Chinese pastors to properly take charge of the elaborate machinery of Western-style church work which the missionaries had to leave behind each time their work was disrupted by China's internal problems.

With the rise of Chinese nationalism following the 1911 revolution, anti-foreign and anti-Christian sentiments seemed to reach new heights, erupting in demonstrations and riots. But that did not stop the rapid growth of the church. Statistics showing the increase in numbers of Christians during those years are quite impressive.

During that period, the church in China was seriously weakened by the conflict between missionary groups with liberal theological beliefs and those who held fast to the evangelical faith. There were also doctrinal divisions regarding less important matters. The carry over of Western denominational divisions to China was unnecessary and tragic. It became not only a source of confusion to Chinese believers but a later point of attack by the Communist government. In order to avoid clashes caused by different denominational structures, mission agencies worked out arrangements among themselves whereby one particular area would be occupied by missionaries from the same denomination. We can understand that from China's viewpoint this looked suspiciously like "carving up" China's land for foreign domination. This unnecessarily added to the bewilderment of Chinese believers and obliged them to take sides denominationally and adopt attitudes of "I am of Paul. . .I am of Cephas. . . ."

Dissatisfaction with foreign missionary organizations was one reason for the rise of numbers of independent Chinese churches and indigenous expressions of the Christian faith. These usually did not conform to Western missionary patterns and traditions. Some Western missionaries were not as sensitive as they should have been to the need and authenticity of developing truly indigenous expressions of Chinese Christian faith.

Pluses and minuses

With the benefit of hindsight, of course we can see flaws in the missionary enterprise. Let us not overlook the significant successes and many positive aspects. Because missionary work has been painted so heroically, to achieve a balance I have taken the liberty of conceding some weaknesses. We need to be realistic in assessing history so that we may understand China's apprehension, persisting to the present, toward Western or foreign missions.

Missionaries sincerely answered what they believed was the call of God to leave comfortable homes and familiar surroundings to carry out the Great Commission of our Lord. They endured great hardships and left behind many graves of loved ones on the hillsides of China. Most of them tried to identify with the Chinese, truly loved them, and many laid down their lives to bring them the gospel. Missionaries translated the Scriptures and other basic Christian literature into the Chinese language. They made significant strides toward training a Chinese clergy and most of them sincerely wanted to foster a truly Chinese church. Yes, they did reflect the culture from which they came, and too often equated or confused aspects of their Western civilization with the biblical standard. Despite their foreignness, which they could not help, their shortcomings, which were usually innocent, and their failures, which often were not their fault, *God used them mightily to plant the gospel seed in China.*

The good seed grew!

It was unfortunate that social, political, cultural, and economic fuzz surrounded the introduction of the gospel to the Chinese people. Missionaries were caught in the web of their times, as we are in our generation. But God is sovereign. What He begins He accomplishes—through us, in spite of us, or without us! The Lord uses whatever willing hearts and hands are available to Him in His worldwide harvest field.

To God be the glory! Christian roots did make their way down into the good earth of China and the Chinese church sprouted upward expressing life in Christ. The Church of Jesus Christ was firmly planted and began to be watered by persecution. At great cost to themselves, and braving the misunderstanding of their countrymen, many Chinese people genuinely accepted Christ as their Savior and Lord and proceeded to serve Him faithfully despite persecution. Two hundred and fifty missionaries lost their lives in the Boxer Rebellion. But let us not forget that 40,000 Chinese believers were also killed. Some Chinese Christians remained associated with the foreign missionary enterprise, while others established uniquely indigenous expressions of New Testament Church life.

The noose tightens

When the Communists first came to power in the so-called "Liberation" of 1949, they did not immediately disrupt religious activities. By that year, 20,000 Protestant churches had been established with approximately 840,000 converts. That represented less than 0.25 percent of the population at that time. The foreign missionary force numbered 5,600 missionaries, reinforced by 8,500 Chinese evangelists, 3,500 Bible women, and 2,100 ordained Chinese pastors.

But the government gradually began to exercise control over churches by establishing the Religious Affairs Bureau in 1951. Each of the major religions in China came under a separate organization. For the Christians it was two-fold: the Protestant Three-Self Patriotic Movement, and the Catholic National Patriotic Association, the latter to supervise the over 3 million Catholics, who at that time had about 3,000 each of foreign priests and Chinese priests. Other religious groups in China, like the Buddhists and Muslims, each had a government organization to supervise them.

The Three-Self principles, which required that all Chinese churches should be self-supporting, self-propagating, and self-governing, were a reaction against any kind of foreign domination. These

121

principles were not new, and in fact were stated goals of early mission- aries. The leadership of this state-controlled movement was not neces- sarily even religious, but made up of persons who were on the government's payroll and would be sure to carry out the Communist Party line. Many sincere Chinese Christians opposed any connection with the Three-Self movement, labeling it a compromising body and shunning the pastors connected with it as liberals, informants, and political puppets. That early period still represented a Communist "soft line" toward religion.

God had uniquely prepared some of the indigenous Christian groups to face the coming threat of Communism. They were free from foreign control and funds from their inception, usually biblically sound and evangelistic, sometimes, but not always, pentecostal in worship and ministry. Some were communal in lifestyle, generally without tradi- tional Western-style church buildings. They were non-denominational, strong in lay ministry, and family oriented. In the beginning, govern- ment pressures didn't disturb them greatly because their structures were de-centralized, their spiritual expression was grassroots Chinese and contextualized, and they were *already* functioning according to the Three-Self principles in a natural New Testament way.

On the other hand, Chinese churches that were more closely aligned with the structures of the West and associated with the foreign missionary enterprise did not fare as well when persecution came and traditional buildings and clergy and church programs were snatched from them.

Inevitably, the hard line

Before long the "hard line" fell upon all foreigners in China including merchants and missionaries. British and American tradesmen had dominated China's trade from the turn of the century and reaped high profits. Their property and possessions in China were enormous. Many foreign mission agencies, especially denominational ones, also had considerable properties, huge investments and holdings. The Communists fanned the fire of anti-Western feelings and ousted both groups, sweeping out thousands of missionaries and religious represen- tatives.

Most of the missionaries had earnestly been trying to turn over church leadership to the Chinese Christians, but the undercurrent of foreignness and Western traditions seemed to hinder the process. In the early 1950s, Chinese Christians were pressured to cut all connections with missionaries and refuse any financial support from the West. Roman Catholics were a prime target because of their integral relationship with a foreign spiritual hierarchy with its anti-communist position in Rome. Some churches remained nominally open but under state control until about 1966.

The great dragnet

In other chapters I have described the catastrophe of the "Cultural Revolution." Covering the years 1966-76, its target was all bourgeois persons in China, her own people, her intellectuals, the educated, and anyone with a connection to the "imperialistic West." It turned against China's own ancient established traditions and ethics, her own classic history, "superstitions" of every stripe, and all religious structures.

Especially during 1967-68 inconceivable devastation took place as the youthful "Red Guards" ruthlessly smashed museums, temples, cultural objects, historical artifacts, and churches. They indiscriminately burned large quantities of priceless and irreplaceable books and documents. Frenzied youths tortured and killed their own countrymen at random. During this period Christian churches were closed, public worship and evangelism were forbidden, and Chinese Christians were subjected to great suffering. It is doubtful if China will ever recover fully from this havoc.

Survival tactics

From that point on, clandestine home gatherings or "house churches" became the sole vehicle for the survival of Christianity in China. Christians met in the pattern of the Early Church when believers gathered in homes. Christians were mentally and physically persecuted as "anti-revolutionaries" and sent to labor camps or to the countryside for "re-education." Even Christians who had been willing to align themselves with the Three-Self movement were not exempt. The Bible became an illegal book and was confiscated and burned. Countless thousands of Chinese Christians were tortured and killed because they would not renounce their faith.

Let us remember that the force of opposition was directed not only at Christians but against *all* religions, against intellectuals, and all progressive thinkers in China who were not openly revolutionary. Christians suffered by association.

The persecutions of the "Cultural Revolution" served to separate genuine Christian believers from the counterfeit or nominal adherents. It was inevitable that some Chinese Christians would compromise because they could not endure the intense pressures and persecution. Some were driven to suicide. Others, under torture and brute force, betrayed fellow believers.

But it is well documented by our personal contacts and information from countless believers and groups in China that many, many thousands remained faithful even unto death, aggressively witnessing for Christ and winning converts in spite of being imprisoned, sent to labor camps. *The gates of hell did not prevail* against those Christian Chinese who were truly God's own children, born again directly from above! O

The Church Triumphant

What are Christians like in China? The answers are as diverse as if we were asked to describe Christians in America. Youthful new converts in China have different characteristics from elderly believers who struggled through prison experiences and political upheavals. Rural believers are not like urban Christians. Those in city churches registered with the government are different from believers worshipping primarily in homes.

Nevertheless, I will attempt some generalizations based on similarities of background, faith, manner of worship, and common conditions throughout the provinces of China. I will round out the picture from personal experience and from information compiled by Christian research centers. A vibrant, common faith in Jesus Christ is the invisible bond uniting them as Christians wherever they are. Again the statement applies, "Whatever we say is true somewhere but not everywhere."

After the missionary exodus

Before attempting to describe China's believers today, let us pick up the story of what happened to the Christian church after nearly all foreign missionaries were expelled from China around 1949. I have alluded to some of these facts before, but in this chapter I shall try to put it all together.

Many Christians in the West are still unaware of the enormous church growth that has taken place in Communist China—unprecedented in the history of the Church worldwide since the Day of

Pentecost, A.D. 33. Tony Lambert in his recent book, *The Resurrection of the Chinese Church*, stated, "China may now have the second largest community of evangelical Christians in the world (after the U.S.)."

Few dreamed that the comparatively small number of Christian believers that resulted from more than 150 years of missionary work in China could survive a totalitarian regime, bloody revolutions, repeated purges and persecution, imprisonments, and indignities. But from less than a million Protestant Christians in China before the Communist takeover, there are possibly more than 50 million believers today!

Chairman Mao declared in the heyday of China's revolution that "religion, together with all superstition and unscientific thinking, is stamped out in China." Many mission leaders and China observers in the West reluctantly conceded that the Church might not have withstood such fiery trials.

Sowing with tears and blood

The opposite was true. A groundswell of Christian faith was taking place in China behind the door that closed after the faithful missionaries left. Locked church doors, burned Bibles, arrests and martyrdom of pastors and lay Christians, banishment to labor camps, and inconceivable personal suffering did not exterminate the invisible, supernatural church in China. Jesus said, "I will build my church and the gates of hell will not prevail against it." Christians put their lives on the line claiming His promise, and the blood of martyrs seeded the church.

Back to basics

The Christian faith was stripped down to basics without the traditional Western trappings of buildings for worship, clergy, public meetings, seminaries, Sunday Schools, and, in most cases, without Bibles. But the gospel began to spread by the most effective evangelistic method: one-to-one personal witness. When Chinese believers were sent to labor camps in remote provinces, they accepted the sentence as a commission from God to spread the gospel there. Unevangelized regions of China blossomed with hundreds of thousands of converts. As in the days of the Early Church, "those who had been scattered went everywhere preaching the word" (Acts 8:4).

Why has the Chinese church grown so dramatically without the presence of foreign missionaries? Rev. David Wang pointed out several reasons in the March/April 1992 issue of *Asian Report.*

> We must give credit to early missionaries who labored, bled and died sowing the seeds of the gospel. Some of the seeds have laid dormant for many years. But they did take root. As God's time comes upon this continent, they are now bearing fruit. Aided by signs, wonders and miracles, some are bearing a hundred fold! God is raising up excellent indigenous leadership that is now evangelizing. . . and bringing in a great harvest. Persecution and suffering inflicted by communist or atheist regimes. . . have enhanced the Church's growth even further. Ultimately, it seems to be God's sovereign plan; He seems to have a timetable, and now is the time for the Asian Church to experience revival, renewal, growth and expansion. *It is God's time for this continent.*

With that background in mind, let us try to take some snapshots of Christian believers in China, particularly those worshipping in the house churches.

All in the family

The normal, basic unit of China's society is still the family in spite of the intense efforts of the Communist government to disintegrate it for political purposes. Granted, it may be a nuclear unit now—mother, father and preferably one child. Sometimes it includes a grandparent or two. It is divested of multiple sets of aunts, uncles, cousins and peripheral relatives as was common before the Communist regime came to power. But the Chinese family is surviving regardless of outside pressures.

When believers gather in the setting of a home, however humble, it is in a non-threatening, private environment. People coming and going to a home don't attract attention unless great numbers are involved. As in the days of the Early Church, home gatherings are normal for "brothers and sisters" and such warm social structures endure when other structures fail.

We have largely lost this precious practice in the West in favor of usually going out of our homes for worship, instruction in the Word, and fellowship with other believers.

In Christ, neither male nor female

China's believers don't call special church conferences and leadership meetings to debate whether women should be allowed to preach. "Bible women" were trained in Christian schools and local churches during early missionary days, and faithfully devoted their lives to reach people in home and village evangelism.

During the hottest times of Christian persecution in past decades, godly women shouldered the responsibility of witness and helped churches survive and grow. When the government removed Chinese clergy and leaders from their congregations, imprisoned them, sent them to labor camps, or killed them, women carried on. They could continue unobtrusively where men would have been more conspicuous. Believing women visited from home to home, helped the weak, prayed for the sick, preached the gospel in family circles, won and nurtured new converts, and taught the illiterate to read the Scriptures. China's church has always found the prominent ministry of women in line with God's Word.

Gossiping the gospel

Among the 100 million senior citizens in China, many are Christians. We have already seen that when the customary early retirement age is reached, Chinese believers consider it an opportunity to devote more time to God's work. Since the government encourages the elderly to live with their children and care for grandchildren while both parents work, elderly Christians are in an unique position to influence their grandchildren for Christ despite an atheistic culture. They also witness to their peers whom they encounter daily in their neighborhood, in parks, markets, on the street, and in the tea house.

They "gossip the gospel" everywhere—in villages, rural areas, big cities. They enjoy more mobility because they are no longer tied to a work place, and officials pay little attention to them.

We have seen in a previous chapter that Chinese Christians who were cast into prison in their prime, if they survived, became senior saints seasoned by suffering. Since Bible schools and seminaries in China were closed for over 30 years, and not enough new leadership for churches has been trained, most of the pastors and Christian workers in the registered churches are elderly. They have paid their hardship dues.

As Western Christians in a youth-oriented culture, are we not too quick to overlook the potential of elderly believers? Let's learn from Chinese believers to recognize and respect their strategic position in promoting church growth.

Timothy practice

If the statistics are anywhere near accurate that thousands in China accept Christ *each day*, many young believers are swelling the ranks both of the registered churches and the house churches. Christians between ages 18 and 30 comprise an estimated 30 percent of all believers in China. It is urgent for them to be taught the basics of Christian faith and practice. Elderly pastors exclaim, "Formerly, shepherds sought the sheep—now sheep are looking for shepherds!" The Church in China is not trying to figure out how to stimulate church growth, but how to keep up with it.

News Network International, May 17, 1990 reported one house church leader in Beijing as saying that the challenges facing the Chinese church in the nineties will not have anything to do with questions of relationship to the state, as large as those issues loom now. The challenge will be how to cope with the undiscipled millions of new converts. He added, "*Evangelism* is not a problem—Chinese people are so hungry for God; *persecution* is not a problem—Chinese Christians are used to it; *but discipling is a problem*. China's church does not have the resources to do it."

Young converts are eager for the truth since they are disillusioned with the government and disappointed with materialism. They need solid biblical instruction. With the continued scarcity of Scriptures and lack of trained Christian leaders, strange and deviant teachings sometimes lure converts astray, especially the young.

Unlike the situation in the West, China's cultural tradition discourages youth from assuming leadership positions too early, whether in politics, in society at large, or in the Body of Christ. Yet because of the leadership shortage, we find young people leading large groups of Christians and trying to fill those leadership gaps. They are valiantly attempting to nurture others in the Word, even though they lack maturity themselves.

Our attitude should line up with Paul's toward Timothy, "Let no one look down on your youthfulness" (1 Tim. 4:12). Let us pray for those multitudes of young sheep that they will find faithful shepherds to follow, and that the young shepherds who are already leading whole flocks will become grounded in the Word of God and not lead others astray.

A fearless stance

China's believers, especially older Christians, are not cowards, nor are they ashamed to witness in a hostile culture. They have known opposition and persecution for a whole lifetime. They are incredibly bold in situations they know are dangerous. They don't count their lives dear because so many have already gone through intense suffering—whom or what then should they fear? In the face of government regulations against itinerant evangelism, against teaching of doctrines that aren't in harmony with the Marxist world view, against meeting in unauthorized places, against receiving Scriptures from sources other than the registered churches, against preaching unless ordained by registered churches, grass-roots believers persist in obeying God rather than man. It is not that they deliberately want to be civilly disobedient, but they recognize a higher power than the state.

Prison holds no terror for them, although conditions are deplorable. Some do not survive the suffering and succumb to the tortures and afflictions, but many remain faithful unto death.

God's "mobile units"

The ministry of believers who become itinerant evangelists has been crucial to the spread of the gospel throughout China. The vast distances involved and the lack of a formal network linking house church Christians has given rise to a powerful mobilization of the laity. The love of Christ compels and propels ordinary (yet truly extraordinary) Christians to cheerfully walk or bike for hours to remote villages, through deep snow or mud, to cross mountains and rivers, and to sleep wherever they are when darkness comes.

An article in *Asian Report,* May/June 1992, titled "How Can We Stop?" described the background of these anonymous and unobtrusive servants of God.

> This ministry of the itinerant evangelists began about fourteen years ago when the Chinese government first opened the gates of prisons and labor camps to let out surviving Christian pastors and Bible women. At that time these senior saints were the only ones who had Bible teaching. Defying failing health and rugged road conditions in China, these men and women in their sixties and seventies boldly went from village to village, evangelizing and nurturing new believers. Since then God has raised up a new generation of itinerant pastors and preachers.
>
> These new and younger servants and handmaidens come in all shapes and sizes. They range from sixteen to sixty. Some are farmers and factory workers, some are school teachers or housewives. Their ministry is demanding as they are constantly on the move, preaching and harvesting souls. . . . To us looking on, they are an inspiration in faith and zeal.

The Chinese government continues to lash out specifically against these itinerant evangelists recognizing that they are instrumental to the widespread growth of the Christian church. In their efforts to stop traveling evangelists, the government has insisted that preachers must be licensed only by the registered churches, and that their parish must be limited to one designated locality. Nevertheless, the number of itinerant evangelists, both men and women, continues to increase. They are enthusiastically welcomed by house church Christians, many without leaders or pastors, who rely solely upon these "circuit riders" or walkers for encouragement and biblical instruction.

132

Simple lifestyle

Chinese believers generally have little of this world's goods, though many might have been quite well off before the Communist era. Because they have little, they aren't weighed down with the material. It costs a lot to live simply. By and large, we haven't learned that virtue in the West. Most of us would have a great struggle to reduce ourselves to a simple lifestyle. Chinese believers struggle just to survive.

I have already dealt with the biblical view of materialism in a previous chapter. Poverty doesn't necessarily lead to spirituality, but a lack of bondage to things of this world frees one to concentrate on eternal matters.

Generosity

Despite their lack of material goods, believers, especially in villages and rural areas, are remarkably generous. When other members of the Christian community suffer, when disasters strike, when a pastor or the head of a family is imprisoned for his faith, believers rally to care for the family's needs. We never saw a collection plate passed in a house church, but we were told that believers privately network to assist one another, and also help those to whom they seek to witness.

Many of the house church leaders have jobs, but where they devote themselves entirely to ministry, local believers support them. Because shepherds live on the same standard as the flock among whom they serve, that financial burden isn't great.

When itinerant evangelists come to a village to minister, believers care for them and supply the needs for their onward journey. Does that sound like the Early Church? In our personal experience of receiving hospitality as strangers in their midst, they always insisted on giving us their best. They didn't ask or expect anything from us, but blessed us with their joy in giving.

With all supplication and prayer

Prayer appears to be such a natural practice for China's Christians. They bring all things to the Lord, and pray with an urgency and fervency that assures you they are touching God. They also pray for needs beyond their group and for other believers at a distance. In some gatherings everyone prays aloud simultaneously, not individually in turn, as they do in many parts of the world.

When a prayer meeting is called, they concentrate on prayer and don't usually set a time limit like we do in the West. Nor do they waste time on peripheral matters or arguing doctrines to divert them from spending most of the time in prayer. Tony Lambert, in his book already cited, observed, "In their environment there is hardly room for the luxuries of academic theologizing and fashionable skepticism. There is robust and refreshing return to evangelical certainties." After all, God is present to answer their prayers. So they pray.

New Testament practices

In many of the house churches that we have observed, anyone may participate, according to the New Testament model. In songs, Scripture, testimonies, exhortations, prayers, laymen are prominent. The worship is free form. Some groups reflect a quiet devotional manner, others a more vocal pentecostal pattern.

Those that meet in private homes sit anywhere they can find space—on the dirt or cement floor, on beds, on small stools, out on the balcony, in the courtyard, or leaning in at the windows. Young and old attend. People come and go. In villages and rural areas it is common for chickens, pigs, and other livestock to wander around while the meeting is in progress. Mothers nurse babies and informality prevails.

In the registered churches, however, a more structured Western tradition prevails with a Western style church building, raised platform, pulpit, choir loft, piano or organ, robed choir, pews or benches, order of service, and usually preaching by an ordained Chinese minister in a clerical gown.

House churches don't necessarily have ordained leaders or complicated organizational structure that requires much red tape to accomplish anything. That keeps them on a permanent springboard to grow and to reach out.

If Western Christians have the privilege to worship with China's believers on any occasion, it is wise to "go with the flow" and not suggest or impose our particular pattern of worship or order upon what the Holy Spirit has so beautifully contextualized in the Lord's

Body in China.

The supernatural assumed

China's Christians believe in a supernatural God and His supernatural intervention in the daily affairs of men. They take at face value the promises of God in His Word that He answers prayer, heals, and works miracles.

In the West we seem to have watered down that aspect of our faith. We tend to rely on our own abilities even in spiritual matters, and don't spend much time asking for or expecting literal supernatural intervention in our lives. We seem to have grown out of the need for miracles in our urbane situations. After all, we can accomplish many of our own miracles with today's technology and training and religious know-how. Perhaps we don't need gifts of healing since our medical facilities are so advanced and our doctors are so skillful. We usually try to get ourselves out of predicaments by our own "smarts"—so why should we call on God?

We must be very careful not to throw cold water on the exercise of genuine biblical gifts of the Holy Spirit in China. He gives them to edify the Body, and the Body in China needs them. So does the Body throughout the world, even in our own culture, but we often quench them by our sophistication and self-sufficiency.

God is sovereign in His granting of gifts of the Spirit to His Church. Especially when a culture includes expressions of spiritism and demonic powers, God often employs signs, wonders, and miracles to break new ground and show that He is a God of power and healing. It seems that God demonstrates His intimate presence more freely in a dark societal structure when Christians call upon Him in faith.

Yes, there are counterfeit gifts. But these only prove that there are authentic gifts to imitate. What a burden of guilt and judgment from God we might bring on ourselves if we try to persuade Chinese believers that they shouldn't expect the gifts of the Holy Spirit as taught in the Bible to operate today! They know better!

But let's not be naive

Let's be realistic. An attitude of *adulation or idolization* isn't

135

what we should assume toward Christians in places like China. Affirmation, yes. In God's eyes many of them may be more spiritual than we are. But they would be the first to echo the words of Peter when Cornelius prostrated himself in reverence at his feet, "Stand up; I too am just a man" (Acts 10:26).

Nor should we insist on slavishly imitating them. Following their practices won't make us spiritual. Just because they are devoted Chinese Christians in their culture and under their particular circumstances doesn't mean that they are perfect, totally pure and holy, to be emulated in every detail. The majority, perhaps, are still young in the faith and experiencing their first flush of Jesus-love. They are taking bold but early steps to know Him and obey Him to the extent of their knowledge of His ways. Most of them haven't even received their "handbook" (Bible) yet, and are walking only in the light of their new salvation and their emerging spiritual experience.

Let's not be naive by assuming that their spirituality is somehow *derived* from the fact that many of them meet in private homes and not in church buildings. If *we* meet in house gatherings instead of church buildings, will we become deeply spiritual? If we ditto their method of baptism by using a hotel room bathtub, or standing under a waterfall, or being immersed in a homemade tub hidden under the bed slats in a believer's home, will that make us more spiritual? Absurd.

Must we experience prison life or a labor camp to know Jesus more intimately? We would be as misguided to copy *their* outward trappings as they would be, or once were, when they either voluntarily copied *our* traditional Western Christian ways—or we taught them to do so.

The Lord Jesus Christ is our sole pattern and model, as He is theirs. And His Word is the only guideline and standard by which both believers in the East and in the West should measure themselves.

Telling it like it is

Not to expose or criticize our brethren, but to see the actual situation without rose-colored glasses, let's take a look at a few of the problems and weaknesses in the exploding Christian movement in China. It is made up of real Christians with faults and shortcomings like us—imperfect but forgiven by the blood of Christ. We disclose these so that we may better pray for the Body of Christ in China and be alert to ways we may help as God gives opportunity.

Many Christians distrust each other. That should not surprise us when we remember the spirit of suspicion and accusation that the revolution fostered. Even now it is hard to know who can be trusted and who is a spy of the government—or perhaps agent of the registered churches.

False teachings and false interpretations of the Bible are emerging. Some of these, but certainly not all, are hangovers from the divisions caused by denominations, or splinter groups, or cults of former years. Some are even now being brought in by groups from outside China. Because Bibles are still scarce and leaders untrained, such deviations from God's truth shouldn't surprise us.

The true supernatural as biblically revealed is sometimes mixed up with superstitions. Because of the spiritual darkness of past centuries, with folk religions, idol worship, and dilution with other non-Christian religions, the faith of some is syncretic. People take a little of this and a little of that, seeing no conflict in doing so. The Bible is even thought by some to be a magic book, and some treat it as if it were a kind of charm or amulet.

Some Christians who remained faithful during persecution years are now yielding to the pursuit of materialism. Prosperity can bring a lukewarmness toward spiritual things, as it did in the Early Church. We know that to be true in the West.

Some Christian leaders are yielding to the temptation to build up their own influence. Pride and the desire for position are present in all of us, even as Christians. To have "a following" is heady.

Some groups that receive quantities of Bibles from outside China are tempted to keep all the copies within their own group and have been reluctant to share them with other needy groups. Sometimes it is because of doctrinal exclusiveness.

Some Chinese believers are eating one another up in the Corinthian fashion with criticism, divisiveness, and sectarianism. Some are splitting over pet or petty doctrines, soulish offenses, style of worship, or the exercise of the gifts of the Spirit. There is sometimes rivalry and jealousy between groups. He that is without sin among us, let him cast the first stone.

Some who are associated with the registered churches have slipped back into the trap of nominal Christianity, "having a form of godliness but denying the power thereof." They are satisfied with the mere company of believers and Christian tradition without experiencing personal faith.

Some young people attach themselves to the registered churches in order to meet foreign visitors and receive favors, or to make contacts to get out of China.

Our attitude toward distorted faith

Believers in China have experienced a sweeping famine of the written Word of God. Most have little knowledge of church history. Hundreds of thousands are young converts without any religious background. Therefore such deficiencies and weaknesses as I have mentioned above shouldn't shock us, but rather evoke our compassion. Add to the frailty of human nature the vacillation of government policies, and the continued repressive conditions under which Chinese Christians live, and it is no wonder that serious aberrations and tangents of faith and practice have sprung up among them.

Our modern West has an explosion of cults, heresies, and doctrinal deviations even with the *availability* of the Bible and a *high literacy rate*. Imagine what it is like in an enormous country like China without ready access to God's Word and biblically trained leadership.

That understanding should cause us to look in the mirror and humbly confess our own failings. Does it not motivate us to pray with compassion for our Chinese brothers and sisters in Christ that the full truth will be made clear to them?

Christian radio broadcasts in Chinese beamed into China and literature prepared specifically for the Church inside are significantly addressing some of those specific problems.

Parallels with the Early Church

We in the West might ask how it is possible for such multitudes of Chinese people to accept Christ without having Bibles in hand. Moreover, we have an individualistic mindset and find it difficult to accept the fact that "quantities" of people can be saved at one time.

The condition of Christian believers in China in some way reflects the situation in the Early Church. Let us recall that First century believers didn't have the Word of God in the completed form that we have. They did have part of what we call the Old Testament in the form of scrolls accessible only to the priests and rabbis, not to the average person. This body of Scripture showed them God's revealed will through the history and experiences of the people of Israel.

After Jesus' resurrection the gospel manuscripts were eventually added. When misunderstandings, misinformation, and deviations from the true faith arose in the young churches the apostles addressed them in letters that were circulated. "The Word" in early written forms was not available in the vernacular for the average believer until centuries later. Moreover, a great proportion of the people in early centuries was illiterate, not through ignorance, but because public education was not widely obtainable. People were accustomed only to "the hearing of the Word." Yet multitudes did believe and became Christians.

The situation among China's believers parallels the above in respect to the unavailability of the written Word of God and for many, the inability to read it. Yet now, as in centuries past, one can believe on the Lord Jesus Christ and be saved through the preaching of the Word and the work of the Holy Spirit *whether or not he is literate or owns a Bible.* In Acts we read that three thousand believed in one day. They had no "Bible" as such, surely spoke many different languages, and doubtless many were illiterate. The Holy Spirit is not bound in His workings. Today in China the Lord is adding to His church daily those who turn to Him, even by the thousands—and millions.

Of course I am not suggesting that the written Word of God is unimportant for every Christian. It is essential for the instruction of new believers in all things whatsoever the Lord commanded in His Word in order that they may become His disciples and mature in their Christian walk. Though multitudes in China are still without Bibles, there can continue to be a great turning to Christ. As we pray for that, let us acknowledge the mysterious and mighty works of God in China by His Holy Spirit and truly marvel and praise Him! O

__ 17 _____

Fellowship
of His Sufferings

We may understand the Christians in China better when we know what value they put upon suffering for the Lord. They aren't sadomasochistic, "associating pleasure with the infliction of pain." They simply take the words of our Lord at face value that "Indeed, all who desire to live godly in Christ Jesus will be persecuted," (2 Tim. 3:12).

Our soft view

Would most of us rush to enroll in a seminar on "How to prepare for suffering"? Dave Dravecky observed in his book, *When You Can't Come Back,*

> In America, Christians pray for the burden of suffering
> to be lifted from their backs. In the rest of the world,
> Christians pray for stronger backs so they can bear their
> suffering.

Americans may jam an auditorium if the topic is self-esteem, or how to have the fastest growing church in your city, or how to start a bus ministry, or the way to achieve personal prosperity. But a different kind of consultation was held in Hong Kong some time ago for participants of 12 countries on—of all things—*preparing for suffering.*

Sponsored by the *Evangelical Fellowship of Asia,* the meeting was convened in the wake of increasing persecution of Christians in Asia through political, religious, and socio-economic forces in their countries.

Although such an uncomfortable topic seems remote to us in "the land of the free and the home of the brave," as world Christians we must address it before it also catches up with us. Like it or not, the Bible tells us plainly that *all* Christians should expect to be persecuted. At any given time if we are not experiencing it, our reprieve is temporary. Jesus paid for our salvation once for all. But some of us have not yet paid the price for being Christians.

Varieties of suffering

Suffering may not always come in the form of physical beatings, torture, and imprisonment. Society can persecute us through job discrimination, social ostracism, humiliation, humorous innuendos, emotional and intellectual harassment, thought control—all common to an environment hostile to the Christian faith. Our own society is fast heading in that direction. On the other hand, let's not deceive ourselves that we will always be exempt from actual *physical* persecution.

Throughout history, persecution often involved the question of Church and State. Christians frequently face the opposition of governments as they attempt to carry on "normal Christian activities." We may already be experiencing *stage one* of impending government persecution in America at the public and educational level. The expression of our faith outside the four walls of the church is being challenged, restricted, and stealthily undermined.

Writers of the Bible addressed this problem and gave us living examples of their obedience to God while maintaining respect for the State. The solution wasn't simple then or is it now. We must interpret and apply biblical principles with the discernment of the Holy Spirit in the context of our own generation and culture.

Living in a hostile society

Christians of the world increasingly see the political structures of countries slide into atheistic, militant, or fanatically religious postures. Pluralistic cultures can also become repressive. And under the guise of patriotism, governments can use nationalistic feelings or the resurgence of non-Christian religions to control the people.

In Asia ninety-seven percent of the population is non-Christian. Therefore it is almost certain that most Christians there live in a "hostile society." Christians are constantly being persecuted, arrested, tortured, and imprisoned by totalitarian governments. Other religions, particularly Islam, are bent on eradicating Christianity. Communism, wearing today's fashionable, smiling mask, hasn't abandoned its atheistic, Marxist core even in its declining days. Social injustice and political mismanagement are causing starvation and economic upheaval worldwide. Christians suffer along with the rest of the population.

So what else is new? Christians have always lived under hostile governments. They have never been "a spiritual majority." The church's greatest spiritual and numerical growth in China is taking place in a police state despite the government's kindly facade, off and on, toward the West. Much as we wish it were not so, persecution, not prosperity, builds the Church of Jesus Christ.

The above conditions were the basic premises for the Asian conference on suffering. Delegates affirmed that Almighty God is still sovereign, working out His purposes, and actively controlling and intervening in the affairs of the world.

"Ready or not, here it comes. . ." was the clarion call. Global persecution, not only in Asia, is realistically and prophetically inevitable. It would be more comfortable to ignore the verse, but the apostle Paul must have been convinced it was necessary to tell us in advance that "For to you it has been granted for Christ's sake, not only to believe in Him, but also to suffer for His sake" (Phil. 1:29). Christians in America are not exempt.

The Chinese prototype

Some estimates are that under Mao Zedong 67 million of China's own people were killed. Many Christians were among them. Some believe that more Christians were martyred in China in the past several decades than in all of church history combined! Persecution became so severe that many Chinese Christians believed "the Great Tribulation" of prophecy had begun—that they had somehow missed the taking away of the Church by Christ. Martyrdom was all around them.

Did the missionaries prepare the church in China to enter an era of the most intense persecution in history? Most missionaries came from countries where they didn't have to live in an environment openly hostile to Christian faith. Perhaps a course listed "Preparation for Suffering 101" wasn't in the curriculum of the Western sponsored Bible schools and seminaries in China. But many earnest missionaries showed by their sacrificial lives what it meant to follow Jesus. Some lost their lives during times of anti-foreign violence.

Some Chinese who embraced Christianity may have thought that conversion meant advantage, education, perhaps material benefits. They may not have anticipated suffering. When persecution swept in like a hurricane, they felt confused and forsaken by God. A rough road lay ahead.

But God was after a Church in China fashioned in His own image, not cloned in the image of Western culture and tradition. Chinese wheat had to be separated from tares; the church had to be purified and cleansed before it could explode in the growth that God planned. The instrument God chose was suffering and persecution. And grow it did— in numbers, endurance, and devotion to God.

As we met Christians in China in the course of our 14 trips during a recent decade, some admitted that it would have been easier to die for Christ than to keep their faith and hope alive during prolonged years of suffering in prison. Many hundreds of thousands were martyred, and numerous "Judases" were sifted out. The ranks had to be reduced in Gideon fashion before they could be multiplied. Believers hung on with bulldog tenacity to what God's Word taught:

> Beloved, do not be surprised at the fiery ordeal among you, which comes upon you for your testing, as though some strange thing were happening to you; but to the degree that you share the sufferings of Christ, keep on rejoicing; so that also at the revelation of His glory, you may rejoice with exultation (1 Peter 4:12,13).

How can Christians prepare?

How should Christians get ready for persecution? The Asian Consultation offered eight recommendations on how to identify with the suffering church worldwide, and personal and corporate ways *to prepare for our own experience of suffering:*

1) By affirming the oneness of the Body of Christ and cultivating a deeper measure of active continental and global cooperation.

2) By intelligently and fervently praying for one another.

3) By developing lay leadership.

4) By studying and memorizing the Word of God diligently and regularly.

5) By fostering a deeper spirit of worship, communion, and walk with the risen Lord in holiness and love.

6) By adopting an appropriate lifestyle.

7) By creating effective avenues of contacts and communication with churches suffering persecution.

8) By praying for wisdom, grace, and boldness in carrying out the Great Commission in the midst of persecution. [1]

The Church in China learned the hard way, but directly from the Lord. Now the Chinese church has become a role model for the worldwide church. Instead of speculating how our Western missions can evangelize the unreached in China, we may more appropriately learn from her Christians how they have done it in a hostile society.

Conditions for church growth

China's revival and extraordinary church growth took place without benefit of modern media and technology, without flamboyant Christian TV shows, without mass crusades, Christian literature blitzes, door-to-door canvasing, church buildings, or Christian training institutions. And with few Bibles, an aging pastoral leadership, and no Sunday Schools or youth groups.

The great teacher called "Persecution" is under the personal supervision of the Headmaster, Jesus, and lessons are conducted in the setting of a hostile, repressive classroom.

Democracy, capitalism, private enterprise, a free press, freedom of speech and assembly, a prosperous economy, an orderly, peaceful environment—none of these are *essential* for spiritual growth. In fact, such conditions sometimes lull the church into complacency and lukewarmness, which the Lord says He despises.

Jesus lifted the curtain on history's final hour the night before He went to the cross, ". . .in Me you may have peace. In the world you have tribulation, but take courage; I have overcome the world" (John 16:33).

Believers speak for themselves

Let's hear *from* some suffering believers in China, not just *about* them. A letter from a Christian in Shaanxi province stated,

> We have heard a rumor that overseas people are saying there is no persecution in China. We find this hard to believe. There are more than 100 brethren in prison here, [in a remote part of north China] and many young Christians under 18 are under strong pressure from the police, even being thrown into manure pits. . . . [Since our pastor is in prison] our 5-600 full-time Christian workers and 50-60,000 believers must stand on their own feet.
>
> Persecution is normal for us. When arrested we are sent back to our native places. . .and when released, we preach again. . . .Every time of revival has brought persecution and every persecution further revival. The Chinese church has been in continuous revival right up until now. . . .In some mountain places whole villages turned to Christ—not because of miracles, but drawn by the great love of our Lord on the Cross.
>
> Some teenagers want to dedicate themselves to God. Turned out of their homes, they are willing to spend their entire lives in a dangerous, wandering fashion as evangelists. . . .We have paid a great price for the gospel—much blood and sweat, many tears shed, many lives sacrificed, and much braving of wind and

rain. We are always under surveillance...but the Lord gives grace to endure.

He described how their itinerant preachers, with no fixed place to live, often travel at night to avoid discovery, holding meetings from house to house, evangelizing and nurturing thousands of new converts in more than 22 provinces. He continued,

The church's foundation has been firmly planted. Do you imagine that we like this kind of life? It is for the sake of the gospel we willingly do this. Do not let us stand alone in this spiritual battle in China. Help us through prayer.

A special delivery message for *us*

The same Chinese believer quoted above, who chose to remain anonymous, sent the following translated report *especially to Western Christians,* from which I have taken excerpts.

TO THE MEMBERS OF HIS BODY OVERSEAS:

Today the church in China is being greatly blessed by the Lord and the number of people being saved is increasing daily. But wherever the church flourishes, there are difficulties. If Jesus had not been crucified, none today could be saved; if there were no testing by fire, then true faith would not become apparent; and if there were no training, we could not become instruments used by the Lord. If the rock is not split open, the water of life cannot flow forth. Our persecutions are the means of promoting life and revival in our churches.

Recently the gospel [in our province] has once again been greatly promoted because ten young brothers and sisters were imprisoned, beaten, and bound. They regarded their sufferings for the Lord as more precious than the treasures of Egypt.

It happened like this: They started to preach the gospel in one of the poorest and most barren areas. One day they went to [a certain village], split up and

147

started to preach. The power of God came forth as they preached with tears. Passers-by and street-sellers, Christians and non-Christians, stood still and listened. Even the fortune tellers were moved by the Holy Spirit and burst out crying. Many hearing the Word forgot their food, their work, or even to return home. This went on until evening and still people had not dispersed.

The brothers and sisters preached until they were exhausted but the crowd would not let them leave. When the shops and factories closed, employees also listened. Then the authorities moved in, dragging them away, binding them with ropes, beating them with electric shock poles. They slapped their faces with shoes and knocked them unconscious. When they came to, they continued to pray, sing and preach to bystanders.

One little sister, aged 14, revived after having been beaten senseless. Seeing that people were sympathetic, she began to preach again but with few words and low voice. The people were so moved they cried out, repenting, and believing in Jesus.

The crowd marveled to see smiles still on their bruised and bloody faces. Why did they not feel ashamed? the crowd wondered. Where did the power come from with which these youths preached? Many were led to believe in Jesus by their example.

Do you think this is an unfortunate happening? No, this lesson cannot be learned from books and this sweetness is rarely tasted by men. Such a rich life does not exist in a comfortable environment.

Dear brethren, these saints have gone down into the fiery furnace. Far from being harmed, their faces were glorified and their spirits filled with power. The Lord will have the final victory in their bodies, making Satan ashamed. Because Satan had no way of forcing them to renounce their faith, they were released.

This experience inspired fellow-laborers in three counties with greater courage to wage spiritual warfare so that the number of those saved will increase through us in this generation. Let us all make the most of the very short time left and continually do the work of the Lord. There are still many souls who have not been brought home and many lambs wandering in the mountains without anyone to seek and find them.

We pray that the Lord Jesus will place a burden of prayer *upon each of you* and let no one in the Lord be lazy or idle. Strive even more to meet our need for Christian literature because God has placed you in a good environment to fulfill this task. May God give you a heart faithful to death until He comes. All who have such a heart will obtain a great reward.

'Blessed are those who have been persecuted for the sake of righteousness, for theirs is the kingdom of heaven. Blessed are you when men revile you, and persecute you, and say all kinds of evil against you falsely, on account of Me. Rejoice, and be glad, for your reward in heaven is great, for so they persecuted the prophets who were before you' (Matt. 5:10-12). [2]

Any regrets?

In the course of our journeys in China since 1979, we have personally met Christian believers who were imprisoned and suffered intensely. In no instance did the former prisoner—man, woman, or youth—express regret or bitterness because of their prison experience. They maintained that it was a learning and witness opportunity. Nor were families of prisoners angry or filled with hatred, bitterness, or desire for vengeance.

In a southern province we met a medical doctor who was also a house church leader. He confirmed the figure of nearly 10,000 Christians in 30 preaching points in his county alone. Both he and his frail wife endured extreme physical and mental torture. Tears ran down his weathered cheeks as he quietly, though reluctantly, told of their experiences. Discounting his own suffering, he recalled,

My wife was kicked around like a football by her tormenters until she was black and blue with broken bones. After the ordeal she was hung by her thumbs from the rafters and beaten unconscious. Do you know why this particular county is now experiencing the greatest harvest of souls we have ever known? It is because believers here suffered for Christ intensely, more than in other areas. We sowed in tears but now reap in joy. I am determined to preach until Jesus comes, no matter what happens to me.

In another province we met a young married couple, both of whom had been in prison within that past year, the husband for 11 months, his wife for 6. Their crime? Distributing Bibles that had been printed outside of China.

A searching question

"If God really loves the Chinese Christians," someone asked, "why does He allow them to suffer so much and for so long?"

We may search our own hearts and then ask: *If God loves the church in America so much, why hasn't He allowed us the privilege of suffering yet so that our churches, too, may be purified, our faith strengthened, and a mighty revival sweep our land?* O

----

[1] Based on a report in July-August 1988, *World Evangelization*, 2531 Nina Street, Pasadena, CA 91107.

[2] Condensed excerpts from *Pray for China Fellowship* bulletin, O.M.F. Hong Kong, July-August 1989.

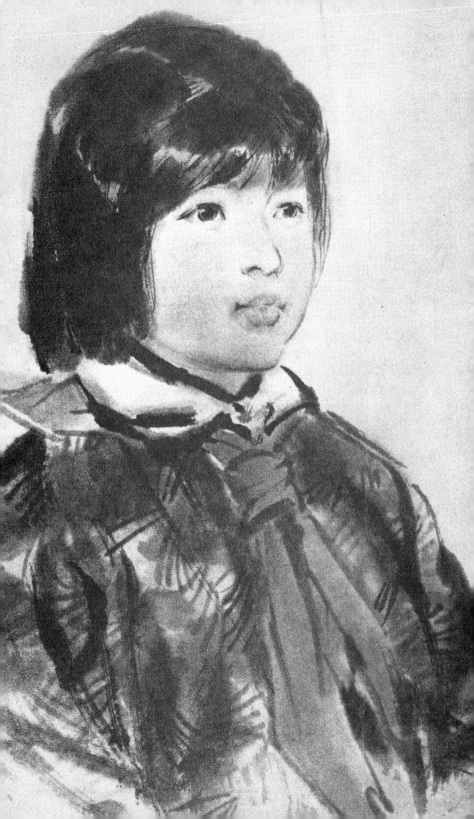

18

Tracing Religious Currents

Despite enormous changes in China in the last several decades, particularly in the post-Mao era, China remains avowedly a Communist country. Her leaders claim that the economic, social, even political reforms are still in line with her basic Marxist-Leninist stance.

That means that the ideological hostility of China's government toward all religion has never been abandoned or reversed. Let there be no illusions that with the lifting of certain restrictions on religion in general, and the official opening of temples, churches, and mosques, China's leaders are becoming favorably disposed toward Christianity or changing their view of religion. The *People's Daily*, a government mouthpiece, still defined religion as "the vain and erroneous responses of man to his feelings of impotence and fear in the face of natural and social forces."

In the *original draft* of China's new Constitution stated it was stated: "Citizens are free to believe in religion, free not to believe, and free to propagate atheism." Notice carefully—this did allow a person to have an *inner faith*, but did not define the right of free assembly for worship, of pursuing a religious career, or propagating one's faith with the same protection under the law as the citizen who could propagate atheism.

Pragmatism wins

China's *new draft* clause in Article 36 states:

Citizens of the People's Republic of China enjoy

freedom of religious belief. No organs of state public organizations, or individuals shall compel citizens to believe or disbelieve in religion nor shall they discriminate against citizens who believe or do not believe in religion. The state protects legitimate religious activities. No one may use religion to carry out counter-revolutionary activities or activities that disrupt public order, harm the health of citizens or obstruct the educational system of the state. No religious affairs may be dominated by any foreign country.

The original clause on propagating atheism has been eliminated. That's good. However, the references to "legitimate religious activities" and "counter-revolutionary activities" are ambiguous and open to whatever interpretation the state or local authorities choose to give them at any particular time. Notice the still entrenched anti-foreign concluding statement.

An article on religion in *Beijing Review*, August 14-20, 1989 sheds further light on the government's viewpoint:

[Chinese religious bodies may] establish relations with their foreign counterparts on a basis of equality and friendship. . . so long as their foreign counterparts respect the Chinese Constitution and laws and respect Chinese religious bodies' principles of independence, keeping the initiative in their hands and handling religious affairs on their own.

Isn't this a good posture to be assumed by foreign religious bodies anyway? It is nothing new. Dr. James H. Taylor lll, former General Director of the O.M.F., reminded us of that in an article "Pioneer and Partner" in Aug./Sept./Oct. 1989 *East Asia Millions*. He quoted D.E. Hoste, one of the "Cambridge Seven" and Hudson Taylor's successor:

I do feel that I can be of use only by being where the Master would have me; and that one might go and do a lot of mischief by pushing into work which the Lord wanted to do through [the Chinese church].

153

Is there a new drum beat?

In the past few years, hard and soft policies have alternated toward China's people with the West and its influences, and toward China's religious population. Depending on the status of the power struggle within China's political hierarchy, this push-pull will probably continue.

During an earlier draft of this book, more tolerance toward religion within China seemed on the horizon. China was trying to show a friendly face to the family of nations and refurbish her tarnished image related to religious freedom. She also needed to gain support for the government and the Communist Party from the astonishingly increased numbers of Christians, a phenomenon that seems to alarm the Communist leaders.

China is anxious to get a favorable response from the West to her need for technology and science and financial investment. If China demonstrates religious tolerance in the eyes or the world, and is perceived as having a growing degree of respect for human rights, it is for pragmatic reasons—the West will look more favorably toward her. The end justifies the means in Marxist philosophy.

As this manuscript progressed, the hard line against China's Christians surfaced again, particularly against the house gatherings of Christians after the Tiananmen travesty.

Trying to keep in step

The Chinese Communist Party appears on the surface to allow a measure of freedom of religious belief. As we look more closely, we perceive that it is not because it sees any intrinsic value in religion, or because it believes that man has rights to hold religious beliefs. It is a calculated temporary leniency aimed at accomplishing national cohesion by enlisting the cooperation of ethnic minorities and religious groups in spite of their ideological differences. China believes that she needs such solidarity to pursue the goals of socialist revolution and reconstruction. To accomplish this, her leaders want all religious and non-religious Chinese people to march in step toward building the socialist state. China's leaders still believe and often affirm that "after suitable scientific and atheistic education, the Chinese people will

154

throw off the various kinds of religious shackles." Communism still pronounces religion's condition as "terminal." An official statement underscored that basic stance:

> In human history, religion will finally die out, but only after a long period of socialist and communist development. We must strive to develop the socialist economy, culture and science, and reform and strengthen our ideological and political work, to build a highly advanced material and socialist spiritual society, *thus gradually eradicating the social roots for the existence of religion.*

Separating wheat from tares

Although Marxists oppose religion in any form, official sources state that the government recognizes a difference between "religions" and "superstitions." Government sources have stated, "Religions are also superstitions, but not all superstitions are religions." Religions, the government says, are distinguished by the common features of having scriptures, doctrines, rituals, and organization. The five groups that China's government recognizes are Protestant Christianity, Catholic Christianity, Buddhism, Taoism, and Islam. Confucianism is not on the list of religions in China because it is basically a system of ethics without supernatural teachings.

Officially, the government neither positively nor negatively discriminates against Christianity. All religions in China *supposedly* have equal freedom and equal restrictions, according to her Constitution. That includes the more than 20 million Muslims (for whom the Koran is being reprinted by China's government at the same time the Bible is being reprinted) and an increasing number of Buddhists.

Feudal superstitions, the government states, must be positively suppressed and eliminated. These include "sorcerers, magic potions and drugs, divination, fortune-telling, getting rid of calamities, praying for rain, praying for sons and daughters, controlling demons, healing sickness, practicing physiognomy, palm reading, geomancy, etc." Two or three of these activities come uncomfortably close to some New Testament practices of the Christian faith, although the superstitions and cults have imitated and distorted them.

155

Religious double talk

The government says that religions will be tolerated as long as they "respect the relevant policies and laws of the government, do not interfere in politics or education, and do not restore systems of feudal oppression and exploitation that have been eliminated since the Liberation." Because religion must not be "a vehicle to carry out counter-revolutionary and other unlawful activities," China's government gives the nod to her officials to continue supervision and control of religious practices and assemblies of believers. The crackdown on home churches and itinerant evangelists continues under the pretense of "orderly control" and "protection of the people." The government policy is still,

> Those illegal elements carrying out criminal activity under the cloak of religion must be resolutely dealt with according to law as must those reactionary organizations which link up with overseas anti-China forces.

The government therefore continues to resist Western-style missions attempting to establish or reestablish some of their works in China. Unfortunately, "false evangelists" and cultist groups take advantage of believers who lack sound biblical knowledge. The danger is that innocent Christians and true Christian leaders and groups also suffer under such tightened blanket control.

Counting sheep

We will recall that the unofficial estimate of baptized Protestants in 1950 was only about 1 million and about 3 million Catholics. Today we really can't obtain accurate statistics for the number of Christians in China. Speaking as a member of the Standing Committee of the Seventh National People's Congress in March, 1989, Bishop Ding Guangxun, President of the China Christian Council and of the Three-Self organization, stated their official statistics as "four to five million Christians, a record number in history."

Christian research centers in Hong Kong generally estimate the number of Christians in China as approximately between 30 and 50 million, a considerably different total than the Three-Self group admits.

156

Because no census can be taken, indeed it would be resisted by China's Christians because of the obvious danger of becoming too identifiable in a still volatile society, all statistics are unprovable.

We have seen that during a peak period just before the Communist "Liberation," there were only about 19,000 Protestant churches and gospel centers compared to 563,000 Buddhist temples. Whenever restrictions on Christianity loosen in China, non-Christian religions also enjoy more freedom—and their adherents continue to outnumber Christians.

On the positive side, the present policy toward religious tolerance gives religion some measure of legal status and even "protection." Given China's attempt to stabilize her law system after a period of extreme lawlessness, and her new attitude of courting the good will of the West, it seemed unthinkable that China would have risked another assault against religion within her borders. But it has been happening since the Tiananmen massacre. Nor did we think China could afford any more religious martyrs to sully her benevolent image. Never say *never*. In China, *anything* can happen.

Too soon for Hallelujahs

To give government sanction to the reopening of traditional Western-style church buildings in major cities, and to encourage Western religious traditions among Chinese believers, may seem somewhat incongruous to us, given the continued anti-foreign feelings of China's leaders. Predominantly Western denominational-style services have been restored in the registered churches of Western architecture. Are not robed choirs and ministers, organ music, printed bulletins and ordered services, traditional sermons, many Western-tune hymns—reminiscent of what China's leaders said they wanted to get *rid* of? The fact is, meetings with such identifiable characteristics are easier for the government to locate and control.

In 1979 only 5 church buildings were open in all of China; by 1981 there were 200. Bishop Ding officially reported in the Spring of 1989,

> Many temples, mosques and churches closed down during the Cultural Revolution have been repaired and reopened and a number of new ones have been built.

157

The number of people attending religious services is increasing rapidly. Take Christianity as an example. There are now over 5,000 Christian churches in China and 13 seminaries training more than 700 students.

The *Amity News Service* reported in January 1992 that the TSPM Conference that month put the number of registered churches at 7,000 with Bible production having increased to more than 6.5 million.

Meanwhile, at the grass-roots

We have already seen that this is not the whole story. Knowledgeable China watchers and those who have on-going contacts with Christians inside China report that the *majority* of China's Christians are *not* associated with the registered churches. Most of the grass-roots Christians continue to meet in homes, especially in rural areas, where most of China's Christians live. They don't want to risk association with the Three-Self movement because it is under the control of the government. If the political wind blows up another storm, they are afraid that they will be carried away in the whirlwind. As of this writing, that wind is gaining in velocity again.

As outsiders, let's not be guilty of polarizing the church in China. It is not for us to erect a fence between any groups of Christians in China. Without question there are hundreds of thousands of sincere, born-again believers in the registered churches, as well as among those who gather in homes. The location of the place of worship is not the most important factor. The woman of Samaria tried to divert personal spiritual discussion with Jesus by asking Him *"Where* is the proper place for worship?"* Those of us looking in from the outside should not fall into the trap of Satan who loves to get us off the track with such debates. Let us affirm the Body of Christ *wherever* we find it, and leave the sorting out and the judgment to the Lord of the harvest.

The key is inside

The key to evangelizing China does not lie under the "Welcome Mat" at the door to China. It may not really matter whether a Western missionary force can *ever again* enter to resume traditional mission work. God can and did choose to work through Western missionaries when He called them to China in the early days to plant the seed. Then He obviously chose to work without them when He allowed them to be forced out.

The key to China's evangelization undoubtedly lies largely with the Christians inside China who are proclaiming the gospel to their own countrymen. That is the most effective contextualization of God's message. If China's Christians *never* receive more freedom than they have right now, *revival can continue* to sweep the land even under a hostile, restrictive government.

As we have seen, adversity is usually more conducive to spirituality and evangelistic fervor than prosperity. The most explosive growth in the church in China, unprecedented in world evangelism, took place under long-term restrictive conditions.

Let's not be so conceited as to think that the Holy Spirit can't work without Western multi-media and mega-methods. The trappings of Western Christianity continue to be as inappropriate for China today as they were in 1842.

Thermostat-controlled Christianity

Christians in China, whether worshipping in the registered churches or in home meetings, continue to live, worship, and evangelize in a society whose religious climate is thermostatically controlled by the political hierarchy. We have seen that by the grace of God believers not only survived when the temperature was hot with persecution, but they went on to effectively evangelize under life threatening conditions. Now that the temperature and pressure has been lowered somewhat closer to the comfort zone, critical problems continue to face them, demanding keen spiritual discernment.

Believers have to make critical decisions whether to comply when the government-controlled Three-Self movement demands that they parrot an exaggerated self-hood against Western brothers and sisters in Christ who are genuinely concerned for their spiritual welfare. They are supposed to say, "Stay away and don't help us propagate our faith. Don't offer financial help to our Chinese Church. Don't bring us the Bibles we so desperately need because our government promised to print them for us. Don't nurture us over the airwaves or by sending us Christian literature for which we are starved. We want to do it ourselves,

159

in our own way, in our own time frame."

Do all of these statements accurately reflect the attitude of the whole church in China? Since no one can reliably generalize the attitude of "the whole church" in any Western country, how can we know accurately how "the whole Church in China" feels? The Christians and their meeting places are scattered and diverse in character, unconnected and uncountable. Who can say he really speaks for China's church with any degree of authority? Certainly not those related to the Three-Self movement or, for that matter, any self-styled spokesmen for the house churches.

Nevertheless, through repeated and intimate contacts with true believers in wide areas of China, Christian research centers and China-watchers can guess that the above exaggerated isolationist principles are *not* embraced everywhere in China, nor by all Christians either within or outside of the registered churches.

A Chinese house church pastor in his nineties, who formerly had a close relationship with foreign missionaries before the revolution, explained to us,

> As for the first two points of the self-principles for our Chinese church, (self-government and self-support) we give our hearty affirmation. But for the third (self-propagation)—the task of evangelizing our country-men—we do accept that mandate, yes. And the Holy Spirit is working mightily among us in China for its accomplishment. But as part of the worldwide Body of believers, we *welcome* the shoulder-to-shoulder help of our brothers and sisters in Christ from anywhere—as long as they continue to *respect the first two principles.* We see no biblical principle that we must attempt to evangelize China by ourselves.

Walking a tightrope

Like performers on a high wire, Christians concerned for the evangelization of China must perform feats of balance on the line of what China allows in religious policy. Like it or not, Christian minis-

160

tries and mission works from outside China must live with the official position in China for the present. When it changes, we will need to adjust. If we violate it now, we are likely to cause difficulty for the believers there and possibly contribute to the slamming of the door for future evangelization cooperation. We precariously walk a tightrope with dire consequences if our feet slip.

On one hand, we can't afford to persist in rash, overzealous, well-meaning missionary impetuosity in the name of faith and missionary boldness. On the other hand, we shouldn't fall into the trap of doing nothing just because we are afraid of doing the wrong thing. Only the Lord of the harvest can give us His balance pole of discernment.

By now we should be able to better understand China's position from the vantage point of history. We've seen that we may have unwittingly contributed to China's suspicion against foreign religion. We don't condone some of her regulations. Neither do we dare pretend they aren't there, belittle them, or stride rough-shod over her restrictions. The Holy Spirit will give ample wisdom, discernment, and creative, acceptable methods to His servants *if we listen carefully to Him.*

Is it not possible to carry on the work of God's Kingdom with courage, faith, and good conscience and not *deliberately offend* governmental authority *any more than necessary?* We can take the biblical position: "If possible, so far as it depends on you, be at peace with all men" (Rom.12:18). As those who are burdened for China's evangelization, we can apply the principles that the apostle Paul set forth in Romans 13. The same principles can guide the Christians within China as they evangelize. ○

19

What's The Weather Forecast?

China is a long-time manufacturer of electric fans. Fans were a luxury item during revolutionary days. In the post-revolutionary period they were one of several early status items on the "most wanted" list. They are commonplace now, even in rural areas that finally have electric power. Fans are one of China's major world export items that you and I see in our local department store.

China is good at controlling the breeze, or wind, in matters of politics as well as climate. If it suits their purpose and strategy, China's leaders stir up cold air or blow "hot air" into both China's own space or onto the world scene. Communist rhetoric can be either full of bluster and swagger or bombastic with generosity and liberalism. For reasons which we have explored, for a period before Tiananmen, China was blowing "a kinder, gentler" warm and friendly breeze toward the religious scene. After the Tiananmen episode in 1989, she turned the heat on again, especially toward believers who gather for worship in homes.

Significant articles in Chinese and English appeared in a number of China's periodicals just before Tiananmen. The *Beijing Review*, March 20-26, 1989 issue carried a full color photo on its cover of Catholics at Mass in Beijing's large, European-style north cathedral at Xishiku. One major article highlighted religion in general, and the other focused specifically on the surge in China's Christianity. The former, from which I quote extensively because of its significance, was written jointly by Bishop Ding, Dean of Theology at the Nanjing Jinling College, and an associate professor named Wang.

Opium—to puff or not to puff

Titled "Breakthroughs in Religious Research," the article stated, "All religions, of whatever nature, are social entities. . .that form a part of the spiritual side of human society."

Commenting on the often repeated remark of Karl Marx that "religion is the opiate of the people," the authors maintain that it doesn't represent the Marxist view of religion, and it did not, in fact, originate with him. "It is also worth noting that at that time opium was used as a medicine to alleviate pain rather than as a narcotic drug. It is true that people once used religion to poison both themselves and others," they continue, "however, this was not religion's only historical role. . .nor even its major role. Religion has contributed to mobilizing and uniting people in revolutionary wars."

Because of such seeming moderation in position, I will quote their comments more fully, as they, in turn, quoted from a new book by Luo Zhufeng, *Religion in China During the Socialist Period.*

1) Opium is principally a metaphor to allude to and illustrate the negative role religion performs under certain conditions in a class society. 2) Historically, changes in the role of religion accompanied changes in social conditions. Therefore, religion should not be indiscriminately viewed as an opiate. 3) During the socialist period, it is even more improper to liken religion to opium. These three points represent a major breakthrough in China's religious research and bring to an end the years of debate on whether religion should be regarded as an opiate. There remain few people today, if any, who still treat religion as an opiate.

Temporary pat on the back

This seems to be a calculated effort to win the favor of religious persons by gentle pats on the back but accompanied by the same old Party music. Ding and Wang point out that,

Most religious believers, whatever sect they belong to, observe laws, behave well and are eager to help others. Juvenile delinquents are scarcely if ever connected with religious institutions. Religion has the capacity to instill good behavior into believers, and religious circles remain active in doing good deeds beneficial for society. Most leading members of religious groups since the founding of the PRC have supported socialism. Likewise, most of their followers have contributed through their work to the construction of a socialist society. Indeed, as far as we know, the percentage of Christians who have been named in many places as advanced workers, advanced producers, or model workers is higher than that of their non-believing colleagues. In fact, it is true to say that with changes in Chinese society, the country's various religions have advanced rapidly and adapted themselves to socialism.

Now they lower the boom!

After many paragraphs commending religion in general, (photos accompanying the article were of Buddhist monks, Muslims in a mosque, a Chinese Catholic bishop, a Taoist priest chanting Scriptures, and Tibetan lamas conducting a ceremony) the typical Party line emerges:

Although the Communist Party of China advocates atheism, it recognizes the rational reasons for the existence of religions...[we must study] how religion could best be incorporated into socialist society and what roles it is most suited to perform. Co-ordination should be based on patriotism and socialism with the Constitution as the guiding criterion; it should not be built upon a foundation of materialism or have as its aim the 'elimination' of religion. In a country with a population of 1 billion, there should be a diversity in ways of thinking. To carry out socialist construction on a scale unprecedented in history, everybody is required to play their part in the achievement of our gigantic goals.

Piping the same old tune

The authors then parrot the Party line:

As it is utterly impossible to reach a unanimity of ideological belief, to launch a debate on the rights and wrongs of theism and atheism can only be harmful. Only if we adhere to the four cardinal principles (adherence to the socialist road, to the people's democratic dictatorship, to the leadership of the Communist Party and to Marxism-Leninism and Mao Zedong Thought) and allow freedom of religious belief, can all the positive factors in China be mobilized.

As all phenomena that hinder the realization of China's socialist modernization program must be eliminated, it is necessary that the country's religions rid themselves of all facets which do not accord with socialism. The new wind blowing seems to be incorporating religion into socialism instead of each eliminating the other. As far as its global viewpoint is concerned, Marxist theory cannot sympathize or agree with religion. But as a cultural phenomenon, we should treat it scientifically.

We may decide for ourselves whether there is a new wind blowing from Beijing toward her pluralistic stance on religion. Or did China just turn her electric fan low to cool off any hot tendencies among religious believers to separate themselves from China's United Front politically? Her Party line reminds them again in a "kinder, gentler" way (instead of prison and labor camp) that *they are all required to hold hands and march together to the socialist tune.*

166

How a pluralistic society works

China struggles in her treatment of religion because as a nation she is pluralistic. Since many different expressions of religion co-exist on her large land mass, she is forced to be tolerant of all of them. Her atheistic philosophy recognizes no religion as valid. But before they all become extinct as a natural consequence of Communist education, as China's leaders anticipate, the leaders must handle religious citizens carefully in order not to alienate them from the Communist way.

Outright persecution obviously did not work well. In fact, it increased the religious fervor of believers and exploded their numbers in *each* of the religions. The Chinese government decided to try the pragmatic route: "Don't beat 'em up; get 'em to join up by buttering 'em up." The government explains, "We are protecting you, (even from each other) and helping you, but we'll have to control you to do that. In return, consider yourselves a part of the United Front, which will also benefit you."

No pluralistic nation finds it easy to keep her people united, especially one with multi-religions. A one-religion country has it easier. In a totally Muslim country, for example, the leadership espouses that religion, the government is patterned after its principles, and the majority of the people are Muslims either through conviction or coercion. Freedom for any other religious group is almost non-existent in a religious totalitarian state.

Our own pluralistic country

In spite of the nominal Christian roots of the United States and the convictions of its founding fathers, the United States is not a "Christian" country in the sense of being mono-religious. It is also a pluralistic country expressed in a democratic framework, allowing freedom for all religions and protecting each. Cults and Satanists are able to hide under the same sheltering umbrella.

Without going into too much more detail, perhaps we can now better understand China and her religious policy. We can also see why the Christian message clashes with that pluralistic policy. Christianity has a "one way" message. Jesus is the exclusive way to God (Acts 4:12). We are commanded to win others, (proselyte them, in the Communist

167

view) which goes against China's policy of protecting each religion from the other religions. Christianity is *not* a tolerant religion. It does *not* accept syncretism, defined as "the attempted reconciliation or union or merging of different or opposing principles, practices, or parties, as in philosophy or religion."

Clashes with the world system

But Chinese by their history, philosophy, and inclination *are* syncretic. They tend to pull out whatever features appeal to them from any religious system and combine them in their own Chinese belief-soup without regarding it as inconsistent. Conversion to the Christian faith, however, puts an end to that religious stir-fry. Clash!

Admittedly, Christianity *is* a threat to any kingdom or government of this world in the sense that, according to prophetic Scriptures, all nations will eventually be brought under the rule of Christ. Clash!

The present citizens of Christ's kingdom, the Christians, owe allegiance first to Christ, and only secondly to any earthly ruler. When the government requires Christians in China to support slogans such as, "Country and Church" in that order of loyalty, or even as equal loyalties, these are not biblically acceptable. "Christ and Caesar" can never be on an equal plane. Clash!

This world is *not* my home

The Communist believes that in the flow of history, society is progressing inevitably toward a more perfect world. This clashes again with the Christian view. To achieve this ultimate goal, Communist governments must keep fomenting revolutions. And if the fires of revolution burn low, they must stir them up. Yes, it *is* hard for any Communist government to get its Christians very excited about giving their lives to change earthly society the Communist way. Communists criticize Christians for accepting the present world conditions instead of trying to change them.

In the past, the appraisal of Christianity as the "opiate of the people," in the positive sense of medicinal alleviation of pain, had some validity. (Of course not in the sense of being drugged into confused stupor to escape reality.) The biblical world view, over-simplified, is, "This world really *isn't* my home; it is bad and getting worse; we expect present inequities, injustices, and persecution therefore let us bear them joyfully; Jesus is coming soon; we'll have our reward in heaven!"

This is not escapism or "pie in the sky by and by." The Christian knows that society cannot become permanently righteous because it is led by unregenerate men. Legislation can't manipulate men to become righteous. In a positive sense, *the faith of a Christian and our hope of eternal life does relieve the pain of living in an unrighteous society anywhere in the world*. Thank God! At the same time, the Christian, by exercising God's power from within, and His wisdom from without, can and should affect society for good as much as he can through personal and collective action.

In the beginnings of the foreign missions enterprise, and doubtless not intended so by the missionaries, conversion did seem to isolate Chinese converts from the distressing problems of society because of the almost exclusive emphasis on spiritual matters. It tended to take them out of the world. God dealt successfully with that imbalance during the revolutionary era by bringing everyone, Christian believers included, *into the working world* to share the problems common to their fellow man.

The Christians, whom Jesus called "the salt," were finally put "into the soup," as it were, instead of remaining in the salt shaker on the cupboard shelf. Chinese Christians were forced out of their isolation into mainstream society where their saltiness would be spiritually productive. O

20

Why Dress Up
To Go Nowhere?

In the mid-1970s, AMBASSADORS FOR CHRIST,INC., this book's publisher, conducted a China mission survey. Because AFC represents nearly thirty years of ministry among Chinese students, scholars, trainees, and professional persons who have come to the United States and Canada, its vision naturally focused on the possibility that China would open again to Christian witness. At that time, China was militantly belligerent toward any outside interference and the evangelization of China looked hopeless.

AFC staff first polled Western mission agencies, denominational and independent, the executives of those organizations, and individual missionaries. They were asked about their expectations for future ministry in China. The query was limited to those who had previous ministry in China or among Chinese overseas.

A comprehensive questionnaire was designed to inquire what, if anything, the agency or mission board was doing to prepare for the possible re-opening of mainland China for gospel witness. At that time no missionaries were serving in China and the blood bath of the "Cultural Revolution" and Mao-mania was in full swing. The Christian world presumed that the church in China could not be surviving and that a century and a half of missionary work had perhaps been wiped out.

The first of the twenty-five or so questions in the survey was, "Do you think China will ever open to allow foreign missionaries to re-enter?"

AFC directed the same questions, but from a slightly different perspective, to Chinese Christian ministries, para-church organizations, Chinese churches and their leaders in Hong Kong, in other Asian countries, and in North America. The answers varied considerably depending on whether the comments came from Chinese Christians or North Americans. With all due respect, they ranged from "the sublime to the ridiculous."

Meanwhile, in the diaspora. . .

Chinese Christians, who were even then active in ministries outside of China, almost with one voice stated that it was not a matter of *if* China would open again but *when*. They took for granted that it *would* happen. Chinese Christians expressed faith in God's sovereign plan and because of His love and mercy He would not leave millions of their kinsmen without opportunity to hear the gospel. They didn't agree with the world's consensus that the church in China had been eradicated. They affirmed the resilience of their own people, their amazing history of survival under incredible hardships, and most of all, the power of the Holy Spirit to preserve what He had planted.

The Chinese Christians who answered the survey, however, did not agree that when the door to China eventually opened it would be or even should be flung open wide enough for foreign missionaries to resume ministry with traditional approaches. They commented with thoughtful insight and courteous dissent that it was *unrealistic* to expect that.

Will the saints go marching in?

Most of the North American mission boards, agencies, and their leadership expressed doubt that China would ever even open to the gospel again because she had espoused Marxism so militantly. After all, worldwide Communism was perceived by many at that time to be on the move and invincible. It was thought to be a menace that eventually would engulf the earth as it gobbled up country after country on every continent. [Note: What mini-faith we have! At this writing, the Soviet Union is no more, the Communist grip on the Eastern bloc in Europe is shattered, the Berlin Wall is down, and the "invincible menace" is being debunked throughout the world.]

Many who were associated with mission agencies stated in black and white that they could not imagine in their wildest dreams that

172

China would ever reverse or revise her anti-Western position. Nor did they think it was possible China would ever again welcome Americans who were so hotly despised and being maligned as imperialists.

On that premise, their predictable answer, "No plan, no preparation for China re-entry." appeared over and over. A few American mission executives commented that if it ever did open, they would "lose no time sending in old China missionaries" because they would certainly "know the China scene better than anyone else."

A few replied that if China should miraculously open, they would immediately try to reclaim their mission properties, demand reparations for any damages, and look up former Chinese converts to see if they could "use them to get our work started again." (I am quoting verbatim because at that time I was on the staff of the organization conducting the survey and in charge of tabulating the results of the questionnaires. It seems wise not to identify the sources of the above comments.)

Driving while looking in the rear view mirror

In an interview published in *News Network International*, George Otis, Jr. observed,

> Most Christian organizations think about the present and the past, not the present and the future. They use historical precedent as the basis for decision making in the present. But that's risky because the current flow-rate of human activity and achievement is such that it is no longer a reliable methodology. We must avoid assuming that our prior experiences are the only, or even the best, means of interpreting reality. Scanning our environment, in other words, must involve more than the act of scanning our own minds.

Using the term "prescient" in reference to Christians, Otis defines such a person as,

> One who sees the future that will be and responsibly prepares to live and minister in it. Seeing the future means nothing if no appropriate action is taken. Con-

versely, those with no detailed expectations for the future have nothing to drive their present actions and decisions.[1]

The church in the West, since it largely failed to plan and prepare for any other-than-traditional opening of China for the gospel, seemed largely unprepared for creative access Christian opportunities. As the world's Christians face spectacular new openings for the gospel in Europe's former Soviet bloc, in the former Soviet Union itself, and elsewhere, we suffer from the same dilemma—*lack of strategy or planning, and confused, perhaps unwise approaches.* Addressing that point, Otis continues,

> I don't think we will return to traditional or conventional missionary methods [in the newly accessible former Communist bloc countries in Europe]. The national churches have many creative ideas of their own [so] I really don't see a need for conventional cross-cultural missionaries. . . .Other non-traditional methods could be employed.[2]

Could not the same apply to China? A prominent Christian China-watcher stated,

> The church worldwide should begin to prepare for a post-communist society involving many changes, difficulties, struggles, and confusion. An understanding of China and her deepest long-range needs as a nation is essential, not a superficial deluge of evangelistic fervor. Such an impetuous, unstudied approach backed by money and influence may already be blemishing the emerging church in Eastern Europe and Russia. Western groups are often zealous to plant denominational or sectarian or cult flags. They ride rough shod over the contextualized evangelism that is already being carried on by the Chinese Christians.

174

We often hear it said that if we don't learn from history, we will have to repeat it. As Christians we certainly don't want to *repeat history*. We want to *make new history* for God. This is the day of *creative access opportunities* to touch China and its people for Christ.

Nearly every Christian regardless of ethnic identity who has the Great Commission burning in his heart can have "close encounters of the Christian kind" with Chinese people. Now that we have tried to understand China's complex history and current struggles, let's explore ways to touch her people redemptively. ○

----

[1] *News Network International,* "Changing Times Call For Prescient Christians," p. 25.

[2] Ibid, p. 22.

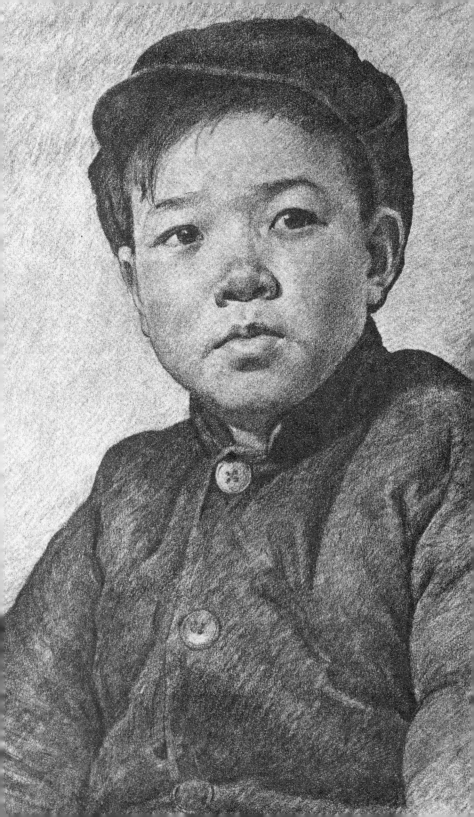

21

China, Here I Come!

Wе can experience "close encounters of the Christian kind" with China's people by visiting China in any of several capacities. One opportunity is tourism.

But as late as 1975, a prominent China researcher wrote, "We see China willing to show herself as a model of a socialist society to friendly visitors, who are treated as guests. *But there is no sign that China intends to open herself to tourism as an industry.* That would be a betrayal of her revolutionary vision and would expose Chinese society to capitalistic cultural pollution."

We won't criticize any projections made more than 17 years ago. At that time, Chairman Mao was still ruling with an iron hand and the Communist government of China was in the throes of bloody revolution and anti-West rhetoric. But time has shown that China *did* open to tourism and, sure enough, the capitalist culture *has* "polluted" her people.

For pragmatic reasons again, mainly for the money that tourists would be spending, China, with dollar signs in her eyes, evidently decided to "go for it." The tourism industry took off like a shot. Tourism to China had been rare before 1971. China's revolutionary leaders wanted to keep her door shut and her house locked to stem the flow in both directions. Her Communist leaders didn't want to risk interference or adverse publicity from or to the outside world. A seat for China in the United Nations in 1971 prepared the way for the gradual thaw in her frigid relations with other countries. After former President Nixon and his ping-pong diplomacy helped to open the door in 1972, study and professional tour groups were allowed in first.

China seriously began to gear up for tourism after 1977, but the eager flow was held in check due to her lack of hotel accommodations and insufficient interpreter-guides trained not only in English but in other languages of countries from which tourists began to come. The China Friendship organizations pioneered in tours with group visas and major airlines soon followed with their sponsored tours. General tours are now commonplace and the average tourist from anywhere can visit China. The normalization of diplomatic relations between China and other countries, especially with the U.S. in 1979, the year I made the first of my many journeys to China, accelerated the tourist trade from North America.

Would you believe?

According to the *Beijing Review*, February 13-26, 1989, China welcomed a total of 4.3 million tourists the previous year, a hike of 13.6 percent above 1987. Earnings in U.S. dollars were 2.22 billion! Tourists from the United States totalled 300,000, and China has said she expects the number from the U.S. to rise by 40-50 percent before long. Besides joining group tours, people can now travel independently in China wherever their interests lie. However, they may continue to experience considerable difficulties in the logistics of independent travel for years to come because of difficulty in language communication, individual arrangements for accommodations, and the limitations of state-controlled transportation.

Gross receipts from her tourism industry fell off midway through 1989 because of the Tiananmen incident. But only 15 months later, China hosted the 11th Asian Games hoping to prove to the world that everything was stable, and that it was "business as usual." She hoped that would help to quicken the tourist trade again. After the Tiananmen episode, China renewed her suspicion and surveillance of all foreigners making it less comfortable for tourists. At this writing, tourists are experiencing some of China's old watch dog tricks again, as they did in the late '70s and early '80s. Casual street conversations with Chinese young people who want to practice their newly acquired English skills have considerably fallen off because the government is trying to discourage such encounters. But that situation shifts with whatever political wind is blowing at the moment.

At mid-1992, *China Today* described her nationwide VISIT CHINA '92 campaign as a record success toward that year's goal of 5 million overseas tourists on organized tours. The campaign promoted 249 state-level scenic spots and 14 special tours, including a trip through the Three Gorges of the Yangtze River and a journey along the Silk Road. It also promoted more than 100 celebrations and festivals. Travelers can now go far beyond the major cities, even to the towering peaks of Tibet and the high grasslands of Mongolia.

Red carpet—China style

Today's tourists represent countries that China used to regard as arch political enemies and targets of hate campaigns. Now they enjoy a measure of "red carpet" preferential treatment. They are paying good money for it. But we have seen what's under that "red carpet." China is wooing tourists to help finance her drive toward modernization, to the tune of millions of dollars, and to demonstrate her relaxed policy toward the outside world.

Let's remember that visitors from the West are only part of the whole. Through the years, hundreds of thousands of overseas Chinese have been going in and out of China to visit relatives. The largest number of foreign tourists come from Japan—286,400 in the year preceding the Tiananmen incident. Hard to believe when we recall that Japan was China's chief enemy, whose soldiers raped, murdered, looted, and devastated the country from the outbreak of the Sino-Japanese war in 1937.

Surprisingly, Chinese from Taiwan have become the second largest group of tourists to China. About 450,000 Taiwan compatriots came in 1988 when Taiwan authorities relaxed their policies on islanders visiting the mainland. The majority came as independent travellers to see relatives, conduct business, or simply from curiosity to see what China was like after the "long freeze" between the mainland and Taiwan.

Not like it used to be!

I won't go into detail about hotel accommodations, food, places to see, and overall services because the reader may purchase any number of excellent secular guidebooks that are updated every year. Accommodations are continually being upgraded by China in order to keep tourists happy. Sign boards for foreign tourists are being installed in the streets of major cities that are frequented by tour groups, and in parks and parking areas. Multi-lingual pictorials and brochures are often available at tourist spots.

China has trained more than 25,000 interpreters and tour guides to accommodate tourists from six major language groups. All tourist guides serving international tourists must now have a State qualification certificate and work on a contract basis instead of a government assignment, as previously. Those who provide poor service or demand tips and commissions, (supposedly forbidden by the government) will have their guide certificates canceled and their names will be blacklisted with all tourist service groups. Nearly 2,000 hotels and hostels, 860 of them star-rated and catering mainly to foreign nationals, are available with a total of over 200,000 rooms. That's progress!

The most serious problem hindering tourism development, according to a recent article in *Beijing Review*, is still inadequate transportation. Tourists become anxious and frustrated about transportation delays and changes in their well-paid-for package tours. Difficulties in getting tickets too often leave independent travellers stranded. Inequities exist—Chinese pay cheaper fares on many transportation vehicles for the same class service.

The Christian tourist

Christians from the West now have an opportunity to see China firsthand if they are fortunate enough to have the funds and the time to travel. Let's conduct ourselves as guests in a host country. What a privilege to praise God and pray for China *from within China!*

As Christians, we are extraordinary travelers—God's special people. On the other hand, let's think soberly and not harbor an inflated image of our importance. China's people are not holding their breaths for us to arrive and evangelize them during a brief trip as a tourist, a short stint as a teacher, or a fleeting business trip. Let's be humble and use our experience in China to become LEARNERS and OBSERVERS so that we can be better PRAY-ERS for China.

As foreign Christians, we should not expect to preach conventionally in China at this time. It is unwise, given the current political scene, for Christians to rush into China with bulldozing, "made in America," evangelistic activities. If we try to ferret out Christians in

China with good intentions to "help the poor Chinese church," we might bring in new "spiritual germs" with which Chinese Christians can't cope because of their prolonged isolation. We have seen that the religious situation in China is ever-changing. All of our contacts in China require special sensitivity to the leading of the Holy Spirit. The Christian traveler is an ambassador for Christ with a high calling to walk carefully, as a wise forerunner.

Nor should we approach China with a paternalistic attitude reminiscent of bygone days. We already have a wonderful opportunity as Christian travelers to GLOW for Christ. "Let your light so shine before men that they may see your good works and glorify your Father in heaven." Let God's presence FLOW through you as you GO, rather than being obsessed with dispensing evangelistic literature from a gym bag wherever you travel. Allow your conduct as a Christian to contrast favorably with that of some other tourists, teachers, and businessmen, who may be giving the Chinese a very poor impression.

Pushers are losers

Rather than mechanically trying to initiate a discussion about religion or devising a chance to witness wherever you go, I suggest that you pray for opportunities *to be asked questions.* The most effective method is to *respond when approached.* "Be ready to give an answer to every man who asks a reason for the hope that is within you." Christian tourists with prepared, prayerful hearts frequently have exciting opportunities to witness. When you are questioned, reply simply and naturally without going into a long theological treatise, using evangelical jargon or cliches, which may go way over the head of the inquirer.

The Chinese people you will meet casually will probably have had no Christian background and will have been brought up under atheism. They may never even have heard about a historic Jesus or seen a Bible. You have a great spiritual experience ahead of you if you remain sensitive to the leading of the Lord.

To share the printed Word with the people of China is important; to share Jesus, the Word made flesh and demonstrated in your human flesh is important. Both leave a unique impression. Lack of wisdom in sharing either may cancel out the other. A sober responsibility rests upon the Christian traveler to China today. Mission organizations are being prayerfully cautious even in informal Christian approaches to China. They are realistic about both their opportunities and limitations. But even a few foreign Christians with unwise, inappropriate, and uninformed attitudes and actions could "blow it" for the present and future Christian cause in China. Doors slightly opening now could slam shut again. Let's be aware that we carry the presence of Christ within us into China as a vanguard that may make the sharing of the gospel more effective by others who follow.

Christian tourists could, in short trips, repeat some of the same mistakes that missionaries of the past (although not deliberately) took a long time to make. God, in His sovereignty, kept China's Christians behind closed doors for over 30 years to purify the Chinese church through persecution and pressures of a hostile and restrictive society. Christian tourists could re-pollute it in no time at all, if not as "ugly Americans," then as "pushy Christians." Good seeds have been planted in China and the wheat is growing at great cost. What a tragedy if the word gets around in China, "Here come the tares!" in the guise of a few well-meaning but uninformed and insensitive evangelistic zealots.

Why a screen door?

When any door is open, not only fresh air and light comes in, but often flies, bugs, mosquitoes, and stench. Non-Christians and Western capitalists, who may be as atheistic as Marxists, are going into China at the same time as well-intentioned, loving Christians. "The ugly Americans will be coming to China with the beautiful Americans (and British, Australians, Canadians etc.). . . ." wrote a Chinese journalist in a Hong Kong newspaper soon after normalization of diplomatic relations.

Who dares to act as a screen door? Ultimately, only God directs the movements of men and nations, and opens and closes doors. But God may be using the Chinese government for the time being to continue to impose restrictions and limitations and thus act as a filter to the outside world. As much as Christians chafe under the controls of the Three-Self Patriotic Movement and the Religious Affairs Bureau of the Communist government, these agencies may nevertheless be God's instruments to keep certain foreign religious groups from coming wholesale into China to repeat mistakes of the past. China still calls the shots. Unfortunately, some of the cult groups have already slipped into China through that screen door and are deceiving the unsuspecting.

In the past, the Chinese had difficulty distinguishing the "good guys" from the "bad guys." We have seen that it didn't help for missionaries to come to China too closely associated with the opium wars, gunboats, and Unequal Treaties. It may be equally difficult today for Chinese people to distinguish friendly Christian travelers from exploiting capitalists who are coming to China under the umbrella of China's Four Modernizations program—or from drug or pornography pushers. It would be easier if we could just tell our Chinese friends that "the good guys wear white shoes."

But I just want to touch a Christian!

It is unlikely that the average Christian from the West who is traveling with a tour group can have in-depth fellowship with Chinese Christians or visit un-registered Christian groups in house gatherings. With certain exceptions, it is still largely discouraged *for the sake of China's Christians*. They generally wish to avoid publicity and undue exposure because of the continuing uncertain political climate. The renewed hard line after the Tiananmen incident has heightened this caution.

It has become fairly common, however, for Western Christians to worship in any of the more than 5000 registered churches and to contact Christians associated with them. We are also welcome to visit the increasing number of theological seminaries sponsored by the Three-Self movement, if we have that particular interest, and if arrangements are made well in advance.

On the whole, at this writing, it still seems advisable for us as Christian travelers to concentrate on the potential influence our actions and attitudes can have on the Chinese people with whom we may have informal contacts. For better or worse, Christian travelers in China leave their mark.

Our learner's permit

Let's examine our motivation, personal goals, and expectations for going to China. We might take a minute to pray, search our hearts, and even write our answers down. Are you certain that God is leading you to go? Or is China merely the next exotic place you'd like to say you've visited? Have you jumped on the bandwagon of secret "Special Delivery" of Bibles because it makes you feel better about spending so much money on travel?

In Hong Kong and some other places in Asia, driver education cars must attach a placard to the bumper to identify student drivers. Hopefully, pedestrians and other drivers will be more patient with their erratic efforts. The placard has a large letter "L" with the Chinese character for "Learn" or "Study" on it. Isn't that a good attitude for us as we enter China? As learners, we will give forth a fragrance for Christ rather than the odor of haughty "know-it-all" foreigners who deserve the former label of "imperialists."

Picture perfect

If you have the privilege of traveling in China, let your China experience be an EXPOSURE—as if you were film for a camera. You should have an optimistic anticipation for what God will allow you to experience there. By exposing yourself to China, the unrealistic mystique of the unknown will disappear. In its place I hope you will gain an appreciation of China and its struggles.

Pay attention to the proper SETTING—be prepared with some orientation. Hopefully, reading this book is a start. Read as much as possible about the current situation in China.

You need the proper OPENING—be open-minded and open-hearted. Don't pack your mental suitcase with prejudices, unfair comparisons, and mental and spiritual blocks. It will be too heavy to carry!

You need to adjust the SPEED—make allowances for your accelerated learning. The pace will be fast. You'll only be in China for a few days, a few weeks, or perhaps months, if you are teaching. Your contacts will still be limited because China is so vast and varied. Try your best to "stop and smell the roses."

Allow time for DEVELOPING—make observations wherever you go. But don't draw hasty conclusions. Ask God to help you evaluate your experiences and correct your understanding.

Get on your mark

Before you travel, fortify yourself by prayer. Enlist as many prayer partners as you can so that you may be "covered" while in China. Pray that God will prepare your way in every detail. Pray while you are there. If you are continually traveling, you will probably be so rushed and tired that you may not be able to have a prolonged daily quiet time. So pray *all the time* and maintain open communication with God. Pray for the people you are meeting day by day. Pray afterward to discern correctly and interpret what you have seen. If possible, pray with your Christian roommate, spouse, or fellow traveler. This trip should transform your praying for China!

Don't be surprised at "Enemy interference." As a Christian, you are not an ordinary traveler. Don't give the Adversary (Satan) an inch; claim the name and blood of Jesus over all confusion, obstacles, difficulties, discomforts, depression, illness, and culture shock. They are all the devil's tools. But recognize that you are *not* in the devil's territory, no matter what it looks like. *China is God's*, by much prayer and claiming of His promises. *And God is in China.* You didn't leave Him at the border! In fact, He was never shut out of China even though its leaders claimed that He did not exist. His own people knew better! God's presence is there in the Chinese church.

Finally, be ready to flow with the opportunities. Don't be upset with changes in plans or regard them as interruptions. Accept them as God's appointments. Don't set rigid expectations or else you will be disappointed. God may surprise you with something better. Keep open to whatever and whomever God brings in your path.

Close encounters with people

China *is* people. Your grassroots encounters with some of the billion Chinese whom you meet can be more interesting than sightseeing. Don't think of China's *masses*; China is simply *multiplied individuals*.

Do you think all Chinese look alike? *They* think all Westerners look alike! In the West we have seen mostly Cantonese people in the business community who have come from Guangdong province in the South. But when you travel in China, notice the differences between people in the North and in the South. You will probably arrive in China with many preconceptions and generalizations, for instance, that all Chinese eat rice. Many Chinese don't eat rice! Because of the climate, Northerners seldom do—they grow wheat instead, so steamed breads and noodles are their staple food. Northerners are taller and have heavier frames than Southerners, who are considerably smaller in stature and sometimes very slim.

To venture a generalization though, some Chinese character traits might be conservatism, reserve, formality, and politeness. They love their children and pay great attention to them, with a corresponding care and respect for the aged.

That magic word and look

Wherever you go in China, practice saying "Thank you!" In Chinese it is phonetically pronounced "Shieh-shieh." Use the term as often as appropriate. Accompany it with a *smile*. Make it a point to come up to anyone who has been in charge of something or done something for the group or for you personally and use the SMILE-THANK-YOU bridge. This applies to girls pouring tea for you from those big thermos bottles, serving you on the train or plane, your tour bus driver, baggage personnel, hotel clerks, sales persons in stores, etc. You have a magic wand at your finger tips if you express appreciation.

English—a "Golden Gate" bridge

Among Chinese young people, the craze for learning English was in full swing by the late seventies and continues unabated today. Especially in the cities, English lessons are broadcast several times daily on TV and radio. English is now required in some school systems and is often taught from third grade. To the Chinese, knowing English is a symbol of progress and openness to the outside world, essential for reading technical manuals and journals, and a step for some toward studying abroad. To practice English with tourists is an exciting lab course for students. The Chinese are building their end of the communications bridge, and we in the West would do well to build our end by studying Chinese.

Chinese young people may come to you on the street and say, "Hello! I speak a little English." Feel free to pursue that with an informal chat. Casual conversations like that in some cases may lead to correspondence and long term friendship.

If you see someone studying an English book or listening to English lessons on the radio, you have it made. Ask them if they would like to talk or read something aloud to you from their book. Listen attentively, praise their efforts, however elementary, and if they ask you, help them improve their pronunciation. Such occasions might provide you with a discreet opportunity to offer them a pre-evangelism piece of literature in English or, better yet, a bi-lingual one.

Sometimes your new friend may offer you his or her name and address and ask you to correspond. If you wish, you may leave your name card or write (very legibly!) your name and address for them. I have found the small return address sticker labels very convenient. Respect their right to decline if you have asked for their name and address. Don't persist if they are reluctant to talk with you. Let conversation flow naturally. Question them about common topics; draw them out to express themselves. But don't act like a government interrogator! Encourage them by saying that you understand what they are saying--or ask them to repeat, if you don't.

Don't feel that you must talk about God and your faith right away or every time. Do you approach complete strangers like that in your own country? It is best to avoid politics or unfavorable comparisons between China and your homeland.

Some will reflect your friendly initiative like a mirror. Say "Hello" or "Ni hao," (pronounced "Knee how?") meaning "How are you?" Continue to be friendly whether you get a response or not. Meet people "on the level" not from a high tower. When you speak English with Chinese friends, speak a little more slowly and distinctly, but naturally, not condescendingly.

You might find it useful to take along a small notebook and keep a diary or journal of your China experiences, observations, impressions, statistics given by your travel guide, and addresses of new Chinese friends. That will help spark your memory. Rides on tour buses and other transportation should give you enough time to reflect and nail down impressions you thought would never fade. They do. O

22

More About Encounters

Let's continue to prepare for our projected "journey to the center of the earth," as China perceives her location and her national importance. That trip may become a reality to many of my readers in the future. For those who do not expect to travel to China, this information has many transferable concepts for close encounters with Chinese friends in our own communities and schools.

We have seen that the Chinese, by long tradition, have considered themselves superior to the "barbarians," as they called all outsiders and Westerners. People from the West, in turn, considered themselves superior to the people in that "heathen" land of China. A writer in *Time* magazine commented,

> ... foreign friends in China soon realize that they are both funny (peculiar) and funny (ha-ha) to the Chinese: redheads and blonds and curly longhairs of all colors and sizes and shapes; hefty executives, buxom housewives and bewigged widows, all big-nosed, round-eyed, redolent of alien fragrances and, by Chinese standards, over-sized, oddly dressed and—face it—ugly!

"Are all Americans *old*?" a Chinese guide asked in the early days of tourism in China. "Are most Americans *fat*?" No, we tried to explain, but by the time someone can afford a first-class cruise ship ticket or a plane trip to China, he or she is not likely to be either very young or very lean." Hopefully, our friends in China have seen other varieties by now.

Long, long ago, an ancient Chinese scholar observed,

> They [people from the Western world] all look alike,

189

though differing in height, some being very, very tall. My present idea of them is ugliness and stiff angular demeanor, perhaps due to ungainly garments. . . .Their cheeks are white and hollow; their noses like sharp beaks, which we consider unfavorable. Some of them have thick hair on their faces, making them look like monkeys. . . .Though sleepy looking, I think they have intelligence. . . .

A decade or so ago, the man on the street in China had not seen foreigners for a long time because of his country's isolation. Curiosity is not as great now as it was in the late '70s. When you tour China, perhaps you will feel that people are staring at you. Don't be offended. They don't mean to be rude. They probably just want to check out what they've heard about us! "Foreigner watching" is a favorite pastime, possibly more fun than watching the antics of the Pandas in the Beijing zoo. Personally I have innocent fun with the stare game. I usually meet their stares and smile at them. That turns a potentially uncomfortable situation into a contest of "chicken" to see who will turn his eyes away first!

Wandering among the grass-roots

If you travel with a group and want opportunities to meet ordinary Chinese people, you might chat with bystanders on the street, in parks, at historic places while sightseeing. During free time you may walk around the streets alone or with other members of your tour group. That's where the action is. Do inform your guide or escort if you wish to do that during other than free time. Have a good time tripping among the grass roots, but don't get lost! Always have the Chinese name and address of your hotel and the identification of your tour group with you in case of emergency. Along the streets you may smile, stop to talk, ask questions, tape record, and photograph. Before breakfast is an ideal time to stroll near your hotel for fresh air and to watch people doing their traditional morning exercises. Also in the evening after returning to your hotel. In the early years of tourism, China's streets had the reputation of being safer than the streets of America. But the incursion of Western ways has drastically changed that. Do watch your purse or wallet!

You may find it interesting to single out a particular age group or class (children, family groups, students, workers, old folks, country people, etc.) and specialize in observing and talking with them, taking their pictures, learning about their lives. They can become special prayer concerns. You may like to make special approaches to some who represent your peer group if you are a mother, a student, a teacher, or a professional person.

Express genuine appreciation for China's culture, literature, books, history, and do some homework in the field of your interest. Acknowledge China's progress but avoid unfavorable comparisons between your country and China. Show your interest in things Chinese when you are out on the streets chatting with people. You might ask your tour guide how to say the "That's beautiful" or "That's interesting" in Chinese.

You will usually have considerable liberty in China to do some things on your own. If you have friends in a certain city, Chinese pen pals, or Western teachers in some institution, you may get in touch with them upon arrival or well in advance and make private plans. Depending on how the political wind is blowing when you are there, you may invite them to your hotel room or the hotel lounge, coffee shop, or restaurant. This is a liberty we didn't have during the early years of tourism when local Chinese friends were prohibited from going into hotels where foreigners were lodged.

Show that you are interested in their language. It is useful to have a pocket dictionary or phrase book in Chinese as a help when you need to ask for something. Prepare and practice a few simple "getting along" sentences in Chinese. If you can learn a few phrases, no matter how haltingly or how you "murder" the tones, try using them whenever you can. Notice words you hear frequently and ask what they mean, swapping them with English words. Ask your new friends what something is called and then write down how it sounds to you, then use it. They will be delighted to have taught you something. Chinese young people will probably have practiced some of their "getting along" sentences in English and will be eager to try them out on you. You can meet on the communication bridge.

191

Along the Party line

Remember that you are a traveler in a country that advocates a different political ideology than yours. If your Chinese friends toured America, they would certainly be subjected to much subtle and well-meaning rhetoric about the merits of democracy and the American way of life. In earlier years, tourists in China were bombarded on every side with the Communist Party line—not in a hostile way, but in a manner that made us suspect that the guide was following instructions from some higher authority and parroting political cliches. We were told by guides and official hosts at factories, communes, tea plantations, embroidery institutes, and schools that good crops, material progress, happy workers, and anything that seemed improved was the direct result of applying "Marxist-Leninist-Mao thought!" Sometimes it was obvious that they were making such statements with tongue in cheek; at other times, with evident sincerity.

These days one scarcely if ever hears such forthright propaganda. Some Chinese people, even on short acquaintance, dare to speak up against "The System" and take what certainly would seem to be great personal risk in expressing themselves so openly. In all of our 14 trips to China to date, no one ever tried to persuade us of the merits of Communism, even when we visited Chinese families privately. Nor were any of the people we met members of the Communist party, or even in favor of its ideology.

If you do encounter the Party line in China, don't let it trouble you. If you like, you may ask honest questions about how the system works, but don't question or criticize the government. The Chinese are our hosts and they are inviting us to see their way of life, not trying to challenge our political philosophy.

Who knows? The present political system may have crumbled by the time you get to China!

This and that

Not only do we seldom meet people who push Communism, but we are finding the opposite unfortunate extreme—many Chinese are looking at everything American or Western with rose-colored glasses. They tend to imitate Western ways without discernment. You may find yourself trying to enlighten Chinese friends, especially young people, that America is really not heaven, that democracy and free enterprise also have serious flaws, and that we have struggles and problems the same as China does. They may be reluctant to believe you, but at least you have been honest.

Enjoy the privilege of being fairly free in China today to exchange ideas about each other's countries. It wasn't long ago that China was a forbidden destination if you held an American passport. You will find that people are very much like you. Grass roots people weren't the ones to initiate the hate slogans against the "American imperialists." Had they refused to follow the government's orders, they would have risked their lives. It was China's Communist hierarchy who whipped the masses into xenophobic frenzies to accomplish their revolutionary propaganda goals.

Sightseeing in China is different from sightseeing in almost any other country, especially the United States. Elsewhere, you generally see places of historical and cultural interest and that's it. In China you have an unique opportunity to visit her institutions: schools, factories, farms, hospitals, workers' residences, etc. You can see China in action. Visitors from abroad would never see such things on an ordinary tour of America. Yes, we know that this is a planned propaganda gesture by the Chinese government, but it has every right to offer such experiences in tour packages. We aren't fooled that the places tourists are taken to visit are typical. Undoubtedly they are well-staged. Let's accept that for what it's worth and approach such experiences without being either too gullible or overly critical. In fact, we are privileged to have this peep into real life inside China.

Do you want to visit one of the communes you have heard so much about? You will find that the commune system is obsolete in today's China. It was one of Chairman Mao's bad ideas during revolutionary days. Communes have been replaced by village cooperative systems with more local administration. Now even that is evolving into more privately owned farms.

More chop suey suggestions

Chinese people applaud to welcome their guests; it is polite to applaud in response if we visit a school or other institution. On the other hand, when Chinese people appreciate a concert or some other performance, they do not traditionally express their pleasure by applause--although Western influence is changing that.

The name order in Chinese is: Family name (surname) first, then generation name, followed by the individual's given name. To illustrate, former Premier Chou En-lai: *Chou* was his surname, *En* was the prefix that all male members of his family would have, and *lai* was his given name. It would have been correct to address him as Mr. Chou, or Premier Chou, but intimate friends might call him Enlai (the new system has dropped the hyphenation).

Women are accepted, in theory but not always in practice, as social and political equals in new China. Married women may and usually do retain their maiden surname. It would be correct to address a married woman, Chou Enlai's wife, for example, as either Mrs. Chou or Miss Teng, since her maiden name was Teng Yung-chao.

Book shops are fascinating adventure stops. Most sizeable cities have a foreign language bookstore that the whole tour group may like to see, or you may venture to visit one on your own. You will see what Chinese people read, and often you can buy attractive books and magazines for every age level in English translations. But if you saw some publication in China and regretted not buying it, Hong Kong has excellent bookstores stocked with literature from China where you might find what you want.

Maintaining a Christian perspective

Our attitudes as Christian tourists should be appreciative, open-minded, and understanding of the dramatic changes taking place in Chinese society that are affecting all of her people. Let's view China with proper humility. Let's not belittle or criticize her level of development compared to the West, or feel inordinately proud of our Western achievements. Our way is no better than her way if we, too, are obsessed with materialism. As Christians, let's keep spiritual and eternal values in proper perspective. ○

23

Delivering At The Service Entrance

Is God sovereign and perfect in wisdom as He controls this planet? The Bible confirms it. He even appoints rulers over the nations, raising them up and putting them down as He wills. (Isaiah 40:23,24 and 41:2) Then it is *God* who has kept the door of China closed to foreign mission activity in China for these recent past decades! The Communist leaders are only the *instruments* to accomplish His purpose.

According to the dictionary, "Whoa!" is a command commonly used to stop horses. But the Bible cautions us, "Do *not* be as the horse or as the mule which have no understanding, whose trappings include bit and bridle to hold them in check." There is a better, more intimate and responsive means of guidance available to God's people. "I will instruct you and teach you in the way which you should go; I will counsel you *with My eye* upon you" (Ps. 32:9,8 NASB).

In ministry, and especially in world evangelism, we must keep *our eyes* focused on *God's eyes* so we can see what He sees. Only secondarily should we consider the circumstances, opportunities, or world conditions. God may work through them or in spite of them or bypass them, but He alone is in control. Aren't we glad that He is?

When God says "Whoa," it may be His way of telling us to pull over, to come to a stop—but perhaps only temporarily. He wants us to look to Him and wait for His next command. When a ministry is involved, "Whoa" may not necessarily be a permanent "No." God may be providing us with a brief but essential period for reflection. He may want to fine tune our ears to hear His voice more clearly. Nor does "Whoa" necessarily imply a "woe" of God's displeasure with our service for Him.

If we "stop-look-and-listen," we may become aware that God's hand is pointing out a "Lo!" to behold a new opportunity or one we were overlooking. But He had to "whoa" us first so we would be still to hear His renewed command "Go!" in another direction.

For example, China's door had been open for us to "Go" in traditional gospel witness with intermittent slow-down or closed periods for 150 years. Then it looked to us as if Communism slammed that door shut for several decades. We viewed that unfortunate period both as "whoa" and a "woe" because *we from the outside* were forbidden to carry forward China's evangelism.

But God was doing something extra special on the other side of that closed door. He used the same set of circumstances to point out "Lo!" and "Go!" for the Christian believers *inside China*. They were the ones who had the real suffering "woes," but God used trials and persecution to purify His Chinese church and steer it in a new direction. That resulted in the greatest church growth in history!

What about foreign Christians who continue to be concerned for China's evangelism? Is God totally bypassing us? Although China gradually began to open economic, educational, and cultural doors again since the late '70s, she still signaled a stop, a "whoa!" to *all foreign religious involvement*. Isn't that a "woe"? NO!

Ramps to and from China

Now God is showing us the "Lo!" of an unforeseen opportunity! China began to welcome qualified foreigners to serve in China legitimately as teachers, business persons, and other professionals. *Christians can enter China by going up that ramp!* That's what we are exploring in this chapter. In the next chapter, we will consider the "Lo!" of China's students and scholars *coming out of China on another ramp* and our opportunity for Christian encounters with them.

The rationale for Westerners being invited to enter China is that many developing countries are seeking skilled persons from other nations to help with their economic, scientific, technological, and educational needs. At the same time, our rapidly changing world—escalating nationalism, the resurgence of non-Christian religions, urbanization, industrialization, and higher standards of education have forced Christians to develop creative witness strategies. Any cross-cultural witness approach must be biblical and relevant to the economic, political, social, and religious situations in a particular culture. Our approach also depends on whether or to what extent government authorities allow foreign persons to propagate Christianity in a given country.

Among those creative witness approaches is the opportunity for committed Christians with marketable occupational skills in some secular field to reside and work in countries like China which are not accessible to traditional Christian missions. We can "deliver at the service entrance!"

Wrestling with terminology

Various terms are used to describe Christians who witness while supporting themselves with secular work. No term, however, covers all the facets of this opportunity. A term commonly used in the Christian community is "tentmakers." That term often requires explanation and may not be a completely accurate biblical word for what we are trying to express.

The term "tentmaking" comes from the biblical record of the apostle Paul working at the trade in which he had been trained. He literally made tents, whatever that involved. He did this, however, only during a certain brief period in his life and ministry. Peter Pattisson of O.M.F.'s China program pointed out in an article "If Not Missionaries, Who?" in March/April 1987 *East Asia's Millions* that Paul apparently didn't make tents because the Corinthians needed tents. [i.e. the Corinthian government was probably not deliberately soliciting skilled tentmakers] Tentmaking seemed to be the temporary pursuit of his occupation for pragmatic reasons. Nor did it appear to be a means to an end, to position Paul to pursue his "real job" of evangelism in an area closed to the gospel.

Acts 18:3,4 is generally used as a proof text by those who use that term. We find Paul staying with Christians friends of the same trade, Aquila and his wife Priscilla. They were refugees from Rome after Claudius commanded all Jews to leave there. We don't know whether Paul spent his entire time making tents even during that period. The passage tells us that he was at the same time actively and boldly "reasoning in the Synagogue every Sabbath and trying to persuade Jews and Greeks" (18:4). In any case, Paul and his friends wouldn't have been working at the tentmaking business on the Sabbath.

We should notice that after Silas and Timothy joined Paul, he "began devoting himself completely to the Word, solemnly testifying to the Jews that Jesus was the Christ" until they "resisted and blasphemed" (v. 6). From that point on he declared he would go to the Gentiles and so left his tentmaking friends to live with Titus Justus "a worshipper of God, whose house was next to the synagogue" (v.7). Many Gentiles in that place began to believe. God told Paul in a vision that he should now preach boldly and openly—which Paul did for the next year and a half (vv 9-11).

Because of possible misinterpretation and limitations if we use the term "tentmaker," I have chosen to use the more straightforward "Christian professionals serving overseas" as descriptive of this creative witness opportunity.

Looking at both sides

Other passages in the New Testament refer to working gainfully while witnessing for Christ and also shed light on being supported while in ministry:

1) We work so that we can pay for our own necessities, as Paul did, probably room and board, and we won't be in need ourselves (1 Thess. 4:11).

2) We support ourselves so we can help pay for the needs of co-workers.

3) We work to be an example to new believers to be industrious and not lazy (1 Cor. 4:12).

4) We take gainful employment so that we might not be a financial burden on those receiving the gospel (Acts 20:34, 35; 1 Thess. 2:9; 2 Cor. 12:13-18).

5) At the same time, it is an acceptable thing to have the needs of the Christian worker taken care of by those to whom one ministers (1 Cor. 9:6-15).

6) We have the option of not exercising our right to be supported by those who benefit from our ministry (1 Cor. 9:15; 2 Cor. 11:7).

7) We support ourselves so that we won't be accused of preaching for money or taking advantage of

those to whom we preach (2 Cor. 11:7; 2 Cor. 12:13-18).

8) We can help the needy with what we earn by working (Eph. 4:28).

9) Churches may support a worker going to pioneer areas so that the gospel recipients would not be financially burdened while the gospel is preached to them. (2 Cor. 11:7-9)

10) Since circumstances differ and situations change, God will show us where and when we need to witness in a more low profile way, and when we are free to proclaim Him boldly and without fear (Acts 18:9, 10).

11) By being part of the work force, we earn a good reputation among "outsiders," the secular society (1 Thess. 4:11).

Continuing service opportunities

During the past decade and more, China's policy toward foreign experts has vacillated, and the Christian professional's opportunity for service there has alternately flourished and floundered depending on whether the political wind in Beijing was blowing hot or cold. We need to understand that we are not dealing with *laws* but *policies* which may be interpreted and carried out variously at local levels by different officials. When hard-liners have been in control, foreign experts, business persons, teachers, and other professionals have usually still been able to exercise their skill or contribute their expertise. However, Chinese authorities try to discourage their close contacts with China's people.

The door for Christian professional service which was opening wider and wider seemed to be on the verge of closing again in the aftermath of the 1989 Tiananmen massacre. Another "whoa!" from God? Perhaps only a comma, a little slow-down, not a period. It provided us with a breather so that we could evaluate our efforts, prayerfully regroup, and prepare for even greater opportunities to "Go" again. In fact, China never did take away her "Welcome" sign for professionals to serve there. Those Chinese institutions and overseas agencies which had established good long-range relationships were able to continue them satisfactorily with scarcely any interruption.

At this writing, China is already setting the stage for greater opportunities. The editorial in the June 1992 issue of *China Today* reported,

> The latest decision on the part of the Chinese government has assured the world that the Eastern giant is going to speed up reform and *opening to the outside world* while building socialism with Chinese characteristics. Reform is closely linked with opening to the outside world. We should open up not only coastal but also inland regions in order to quicken our pace of development. *This will open new and greater vistas of foreign cooperation and exchange in various fields.*

The Bureau of Foreign Experts in Beijing announced early in 1992 that it is planning to recruit *30,000 skilled overseas personnel each year* to help in agriculture, industry, public health, environment, education, publications, and training. China's steady course, though her ship of state has rocked from time to time, is to continue reciprocal relations with the outside world. *China Today*, April 1992, reported her progress:

> Since the 1980s China has turned a new page in international friendship and cooperation. It has established diplomatic relations with 140 countries and is developing exchange and cooperation with more than 180 countries and regions in fields of business and trade, science and technology, and culture. In 1991 China received 33 visiting heads of state or government, invited 300 delegations from 47 countries to visit China, and more than 50 friendship Chinese delegations were sent to more than 30 countries. Chinese cities established 20 more sister-city relations with counterparts in foreign countries, increasing the total to 400.

God has opened a significant door for Christians with market-able skills to serve in China and has kept it open. Will Christians step into these strategic opportunities or bypass them because they do not seem to be traditional gospel approaches? May we let God guide us with His eye so that we can see what He sees—His big picture for world evangelism.

Balance and perspective

Every Christian should be a witness for his Lord whether he engages in a secular occupation or a religious calling. Every Christian should be sensitive and obedient to the Lord to discern His clear guidance for what occupation to pursue and his place of witness. It is needless to debate Christian professional service versus traditional missionary work. Neither calling is higher than the other. In countries where outside agencies have freedom to propagate Christianity, both approaches are valid and needed to give the gospel a balanced presentation. But in countries where political or religious restrictions shackle foreign evangelistic efforts the creative access approach of the professional may be the only one possible.

David Pickard, General Director of O.M.F., in an article in *East Asia's Millions*, "If You Don't Change, You Die," observed,

> The working world is one place where traditional missionaries cannot model Christianity in the same way that. . .Christian professionals can. . . .[They can demonstrate firsthand] what it is to be a Christian in the workplace and how to retain integrity in their career and their faith.

Some point out that the Christian professional's witness is too restricted because he must spend so much time in his secular occupation. The Christian life should not be compartmentalized into the sacred and the secular. When we embrace the correct view that our entire life is ministry, we don't box off our job from what we do in our "free" time after work, evenings, or on weekends. *All* that we are and *all* that we do is included in the "whatsoever" that should be to the praise and glory of God. Time spent on the job is then seen as service to God as well. Extending God's Kingdom should be priority for both approaches. The professional service approach should not be regarded as only an emergency measure when traditional missionaries are not allowed to enter or are evicted from a country.

Witnessing while engaging in secular occupations is certainly not new. Although not by their own choice, Joseph and Daniel were thrust by God into secular jobs under pagan foreign governments in Egypt and Babylon. Through the ages faithful Christians in the common work force have been strong witnesses. Non-Christian religions as well as Christianity have been spread by traders, colonists, and other nonecclesiastical persons. William Carey, regarded as the father of modern traditional missions, declared in 1825,

> We have ever held it to be an essential principle in the conduct of missions, that whenever it is practicable, missionaries should support themselves in whole or in part through their own exertions.

The two approaches differ primarily in the source of their financial support and involvement with Christian organizational or missions structure. The Christian professional usually earns his living in the secular work force. In practice, however, he may not be fully supported by his secular job in China. He may need to supplement his income with his own funds or those channeled through some organization with which he is associated. The traditional missionary is generally supported by churches and individuals in his home country. But neither approach is mutually exclusive. Some combine the two. Both should complement and supplement each other, and both can develop creative avenues of witness. Both approaches require calling, commitment, preparation, flexibility, and perseverance.

The traditional missionary usually concentrates on direct evangelism, pioneer work, church planting and training; the Christian professional generally pursues lifestyle evangelism, personal witness, spiritual ground breaking, seed planting, and influencing his colleagues and others through informal contacts for Christ. The Christian professional's role may be viewed as exposing people to Christianity who may not be reached otherwise. He may be able to quietly lead some people to the Lord and begin to disciple them through Bible study, encouragement, and fellowship.

Some feel that for in-depth discipling it is advisable and more effective for mature Chinese Christians to follow up the new convert. The new believer's countrymen are more in tune with Chinese culture and mindset, know the difficulties he may encounter, and are more permanently situated in China. The Christian professional has a transient status. Because most people in China do not have a Christian background they need time and careful shepherding to help them internalize new religious ideas. Therefore conversion in China often needs to be viewed as a process rather than a simple assent to the presentation of a body of doctrine. When it comes to explaining spiritual concepts to a new convert, a fellow Chinese Christian might be more qualified and accepted.

Preparation for service

It is a "Long March" to qualify for both witness approaches. There is no instant preparation to qualify you either for Christian professional service or for traditional mission work. It takes diligence and specialized training for the Christian professional to become competent both in his chosen secular field and in biblical and spiritual preparedness. Radishes mature in two weeks but strong oak trees take considerably longer. You don't build bridges, buildings, or men and women who are effective for God with "radish preparation."

It is unrealistic for a person with only a secular skill to imagine he can swim against strong political tides and work under oppressive clouds of restriction and prevail as a successful witness if he is a recent convert or his own Christian experience is shallow. Spiritual warfare is involved. The Christian professional may find himself in an isolated situation without the fellowship and encouragement of other Christians. It will be sink or swim. He must know how to gain nourishment directly from the Word of God, to encourage himself in the Lord, and to keep himself in good spiritual health. If not, he will be in a poor position to influence others for Christ. Normally the Christian professional should have some formal training in a Christian institution if possible.

Christian professionals may not be able to avail themselves of the nurture and fellowship of a church body during their time of service. Of necessity, their current ministry is fairly independent of the church in China. Because of the sensitive position of Christian professionals in the eyes of the government, most who have served in that capacity have found that it was inadvisable to worship frequently in the government registered churches, and equally unwise to search out house church gatherings and unwittingly expose them to the attention of secret police.

To enter a restricted country is only the first step. To hang in there successfully in your employment and witness is what separates a mature disciple from a novice. To be offered the renewal of a teaching contract, for example, is one measure of success. Second-mile service is what it's all about.

A covering or a cover up?

At times the Chinese authorities have become suspicious of certain Christian teachers who seem to be using their profession as a "Trojan horse" to cover up their "real agenda." Once in China, some have unfortunately ignored restrictions and become too aggressive or vocal about religion. They are denounced by authorities as having come to China with (quoting from China's media) "subversive intentions to propagate religion and disturb the selfhood of the Chinese church."

This is a delicate area. Motivation, calling, and integrity are involved. As a Christian professional you need wisdom and discernment from the Holy Spirit as well as common sense. You need to be deeply committed to your professional role of making a significant contribution to the welfare of China. Your secular job in a foreign land which has religious restrictions gives you the privilege of being a lamp stand upon which you can set your Light. While you conscientiously carry out your responsibilities *in the honest context of productive service* within your host country's economy or educational system, you should be earning the respect of its government and citizenry. While *earning your living*, you *earn a hearing* for the gospel.

Let's not push The Light. The most effective way of sharing Jesus' Light is not to be COVERT—sneaking around, smuggling The Light, or secretly evangelizing. Nor should we be OVERT—pushy, over-aggressive, ignoring regulations, and abusing privileges. The key to successful witness is to *shine*, not to *shout*. As you perform your quality service with integrity and love you can relax and "*let* your light shine before men in such a way that they may see your good works and glorify your Father who is in heaven" (Matt. 5:16).

How then can we shine?

Since Christians with marketable skills cannot expect to publicly evangelize in China, "how shall they hear without a preacher. . .?" First of all, let's view our service from God's comprehensive perspective. China's evangelization certainly does not depend on our witness as foreign Christians. From the lips of the apostle Paul, ". . . I say to every man among you not to think more highly of himself than he ought to think; but to think so as to have sound judgment. . ." (Rom.12:3). Christian professionals are probably only *a small part* of God's witness plan. Rest assured that many people in China are indeed hearing the gospel through the faithful witness of millions of their own Christian countrymen. China is *not unevangelized* in the sense that no indigenous church has been firmly planted in its soil.

We don't need to hide the fact that we are Christians. Concealing our faith shows lack of integrity and draws suspicion. At this writing, China's government even seems to prefer inviting Christians to work in China because of their record of competence, their sense of responsibility, high moral standards, and evident concern for helping China achieve her goals through their professional credentials. By a cooperative attitude toward colleagues, team members, and Chinese authorities, and by accepting simple living conditions without complaint, the Christian professional commends himself and his Lord. By respecting China's political environment, developing caring relationships, appreciating China's culture, and showing a sensitivity for cross-cultural living, a platform is established whereby the Christian professional may be asked for "a reason of the hope that is within you." To which we may then freely, prayerfully, wisely respond.

At the most basic level, just the fact that the Christian professional is intelligent, well-adjusted, *and a Christian* is a surprise to many Chinese. They have been taught that religion is a superstition, a thing of the past, only for old, uneducated people. Some feel that by witnessing to intellectuals and other influential Chinese in higher echelons, the Christian professional might eventually contribute to the liberalization of China's religious laws.

The Christian's lifestyle can be a contrast to that of other foreigners in China. Humility and a servant heart are not always typical of the secular foreign teacher, business person, or student. The Christian professional has an opportunity to "deliver at the *service* entrance." Is not a servant attitude, after all, the best basis for sharing God's Good News?

Christian professional service in China is not easy. I have been underscoring that it requires strong spiritual commitment and professional excellence. An experienced Christian professional who worked in China and is now involved in an orientation program for others who plan to enter China in that capacity summed up the case for Christian professional service:

> Unfortunately, the reputation of some [Christian professionals] is that they are either good at being professionals and not good at witnessing, or else they are good at witnessing and not good at their professional work. China does not, of course, need more of either of these kinds of foreign Christians. . . .More needs to be said which will in effect integrate professional and Christian qualities within individual believers.

But those who have been stepping through this open door and having "close encounters of the Christian kind" with people in China have reported rich spiritual experiences. Many say that their own Christian faith has become more personal and vital and their lives more disciplined. They have learned to look at their own culture more objectively and to sort out what are *Kingdom values* and what are not.

Opportunities in China

There are a number of current avenues by which the Christian professional may enter China. A major opportunity is *through the educational system.*

1) *The student level* may be the first rung of the ladder for other service. This may involve taking a course in the Chinese language at one of China's institutions. The Feb. 1991 issue of *China Today* announced,

> To meet the needs of Sino-foreign cultural exchange and cooperation, China is taking an active role in teaching Chinese to foreigners. So far courses for foreign students have been established in more than 100 colleges and universities in the country, receiving

some 50,000 foreign students. China has also published many Chinese language textbooks and audio
cassettes and sent more than 100 Chinese teachers
abroad through various channels.

In recent years some futurologists have pre-
dicted, judging from Asian and Pacific economic
development, that Chinese will become one of the
most important languages in the world in the 21st
century. In coming years China will open further to the
outside world and develop Sino-foreign exchanges in
various aspects.

Beijing Review, June 18-24, 1990, reported that according to
the State Education Commission 30 major cities across China now
enroll foreign students in their universities and colleges. Special
courses designed for foreign students have gone beyond just the
Chinese language to embrace 300 disciplines of learning in science,
technology, agriculture and medicine.

2) *At the teaching level,* as a teacher/lecturer/professor of
English or other fields of specialization, you have one of the more
influential roles of professional service. Teaching English has been
prominent, but teachers in the arts, social sciences, Western literature,
history, and many other disciplines are in demand. According to an
article in the summer 1991 issue of *East Asia's Millions,* "The Possibili-
ties of Your Profession,"

Teaching is the one career most widely accepted in
both open and creative-access areas of Asia. Teaching
introduces you to new students every year and holds
plenty of opportunity for personal relationships.

3) *Technology and business* is another avenue of service.
Because China is desperately trying to modernize, she is looking for
specialists in business, in management, in a variety of technology fields
including industrial automation, applied computer technology, foreign
trade, and banking. The Christian professional may be a member of a
foreign company, a consultant, engineer, advisor in development

projects, etc. He may find opportunities in agriculture, food science, animal husbandry, communications, environmental science—you name it, China probably needs it.

4) *In medicine or science* the Christian professional may serve as a lecturer, researcher, consultant, etc.

5) Various levels of *government or diplomatic service* may be considered.

A step further

You may be young, or in your prime, or retired—with marketable secular skills or still in the process of acquiring them. Is God stirring in your heart to pray and consider whether He is calling you to invest your life in the people of China?

I encourage you to make full use of *The Back of the Book* for a list of organizations, books, and other resources that provide information on the concept of Christian professional service and placement opportunities. These agencies have a record of good relationships with the Chinese government and have developed a network of help including pre-departure training and follow-up in China. Summer assignments as well as one year, two years, or longer are available. Many of the agencies place you in a team situation for fellowship and helpful guidance.

A life-changing experience awaits the Christian entering China on the ramp of professional service! O

24

Opportunities Around Us

A mushrooming opportunity for "close encounters of the Christian kind" with the wonderful people of China is right at our front door—down the street—in our communities—and on our campuses. Is God showing us another exciting "Lo!" that many Christians have largely overlooked?

Opportunity has swinging doors and revolving doors. Such are the doors to China. Whether the doors *to the actual land mass of China* are open or closed, God has allowed us to initiate creative encounters *with Chinese people* wherever we live. While Christians have been *trickling* into China for more than a decade to engage in limited legitimate witness as professionals with marketable skills, China's students and scholars were *flooding* into North America and other Western countries.

While we are temporarily "whoaing" and waiting out the curtailing of our access to the People's Republic of China, God is giving us perhaps a *far more significant and long-range opportunity* to witness for Him. He has set a grand stage for friendships with and ministry among potentially influential students, professors, and scholars and their families from China. Has God brought them here because He planned for them to play an important role *in the China of the future?* Of course! "He's got the whole world in His hands."

Escalating numbers

A hundred Chinese scholars started coming down the ramp to the U.S. in the mid-1970s. They were the first group from the PRC since 1949. According to current statistics, the Chinese student and scholar population in the U.S. has more than quadrupled in the past 15 years.

Over 43,000 Mainland Chinese are among the approximately 100,000 overseas born Chinese residing here. Including spouses and dependents, non-academic workers, and technicians who are here on job training programs sponsored by private U.S. corporations which trade in China, the number is considerably greater. Undergraduate students among them number about 25,000. PRC students represent the largest ethnic group among international students in America. In number of students sent to the U.S. China tops the list of 30 countries.

China has sent students to more than seventy countries and regions, according to Yu Fuzeng, director of China's Education Commission's Foreign Affairs Bureau. Quoted in the *South China Morning Post*, June 8, 1990, he said they include those selected by work units who study at public expense and also those privately funded. How specific countries view China determines where the students are sent, said Yu.

China's students and scholars are preparing for pivotal roles in nearly every major field of study. They are scattered throughout our country, living in large urban university centers and small college towns. Those in a position to know have observed that nearly every prominent leader in China seems to have a son or daughter in the U.S.

Who are these strangers?

China's scholars, sometimes referred to as "a new people group," are largely choice, eager, hardworking, ambitious people who are seriously considering their life's direction and China's future. They may be destined for leadership positions in new China in the years to come regardless of which direction China takes politically. Open to new ideas, they are tasting freedoms they never enjoyed in China. Many are especially open right now, reaching out for understanding and emotional stability since the failed democracy episode and renewed crackdown in their own country. Many were sympathetic to the activities of the movement, if not active in it. They are still greatly concerned for their country although hurting, perhaps disillusioned, or fearful of returning to China while the present regime is in power. Some of their relatives, classmates, and friends participated in the freedom demonstrations; some may have lost their lives. In fact, some of the dissidents involved have now made their way to America.

We have the opportunity to take them unconditionally into our hearts for comfort and encouragement. Let us show them genuine compassion and the love of Christ regardless of what is happening in China at the moment. Such intensive care may do more for them initially than listening to preaching from a pulpit.

Tony Lambert in a lecture on "Recent Trends in Chinese Religious Affairs," observed that 70 years after the historic May 4th Movement among intellectuals in China in 1919, we were given a second chance to influence Chinese intellectuals toward the gospel. After that earlier event, Chinese intellectuals moved steadily away from the West and the Christian church, toward socialism and ultimately toward Communism.

> It has taken 70 years for them to see that such a track was a dead end. Now many are much more favorably inclined toward religion and toward Christianity. This is a golden opportunity. . . . But will the Christian church heed the challenge. . . to get involved personally. . . ? May God give us wisdom!

Will they return home?

China fully expects her *government-funded* scholars to return upon completion of their studies and assume needed and important roles in the educational, scientific, and technological development of China. Director Yu claimed,

> More than ninety percent, 22,000, government-funded students have returned to China on completion of their studies and helped close the scientific gap between China and the developed countries, which had widened during the Cultural Revolution. China's government is aware that postgraduates need to remain abroad for a relatively longer time to continue studies or research even after obtaining doctorates, perhaps five to eight years or more. Over 600 were awarded doctorates in the U.S. in one year, representing extended years of study and considerable money invested in them by China.

213

Some will not return. That is a calculated risk that China has taken. At most ten percent, admittedly a small number, of government-funded students have failed to return. Yu admitted that these have remained without gaining permission from their work units. Some have taken out foreign nationality or have married foreigners.

Ask for students who don't *want* to return to China, Yu stated,

> It's not what we expect of them. However, even after they have decided to remain abroad, our policy is to keep in contact with them and hope they may return some time in the future. We will not close our doors simply because a few fail to return.

About 18,000 students from China are privately-funded from home sources or relatives in the U.S., and of them only several hundred have returned. Yu said,

> China has clearly stated that these people are not required to come back and work for their country but they are welcome to return. Every developing country suffers from this problem to a greater or lesser extent. In job assignments they will be treated the same as students who studied at public expense.

What is it like "back home"?

Returned graduates have complained that China's irrational political system and shortages of advanced equipment have not allowed them to make good use of their acquired expertise and knowledge. Yu countered,

> Of course some graduates have knowledge of extremely sophisticated matters which China cannot utilize at the moment because we lack the necessary facilities. But these cases are uncommon. Overall, I do not agree with the sweeping statement that returned students have no place to exercise their abilities after

their return. Our students who have studied abroad should be the initiators of China's development, not the recipients of its benefits. Their task should be active participation in reform, not passive spectating. It is unrealistic for people to want to return only after all the hard work has been done.

China has been trying to woo its graduates back by promising positions, privileges, and better working conditions. Realistically, living standards in China are still extremely low. However, scholars from China may not be making a wholesale dash to apply for permanent residence in America. Even in the heat of the Tiananmen bloodbath, a student from China who was interviewed on American television declared tearfully,

> Before this happened in my country I considered the possibility of staying on to work in America for financial benefits. But since I have seen my classmates and friends die for freedoms in the China that I love, I want to return eventually to help advance those dreams.

He admitted that in the U.S. his starting salary could be as much as $50,000 annually, an incredible sum to him when compared with the unbelievably low $400 he would receive annually for the same position in China.

Since the reinstatement of the Communist hard-line in China expressed by the continuing crackdown on protesters and intellectuals, the United States eased its regulations requiring graduates to return to China immediately after they complete their studies. Some speculated that after the Tiananmen massacre China might draw back from sending her students and scholars abroad. But according to a spokesman at the Chinese Embassy in Washington, D.C. in May 1990, China's policy on sending students and scholars, including those who are self-sponsored, for overseas study, is "an important aspect" of China's policy of reform and opening to the outside world and "will not change."

How about dissident students? Will they be welcomed back to China? In June 12, 1992 the *South China Morning Post* reported that the Foreign Ministry spokesman, Mr. Wu Jianmin, stressed that the government's invitation to students abroad to return home only extended to those who might have held divergent views "in the past" and *not* to students who still maintain those views. They apparently will not be allowed to return to China.

It does not seem wise for Western Christians to deliberately try to persuade newly converted scholars to stay in America. Their impact as Christians in leadership positions in China, tough as it might be for them, possibly life-threatening, would be strategic. Their influence would doubtless be far greater than our feeble witness efforts as foreigners in China, especially in the present political climate. On the other hand, we should not push them to return. To return or not is a very personal decision that needs to be made with sensitivity and obedience to the Lord in each particular case.

Not a homogeneous group

Chinese students and scholars not only have individual differences, they have generational distinctives characteristic of their age group. Please refer to earlier chapters in this book for the backgrounds of each of the categories of China's population. In recent years, those who are coming to America are even more diverse in background, age, and fields of study. Because China was isolated for so many years, the majority who arrived here in the late '70s and early '80s were older scholars, researchers, and professors. Recent arrivals include a mid-group in their late thirties and forties and a definitely younger undergraduate category of students in their twenties. About 80 percent are men.

In summary, the older group was educated before or during the early Communist period and some previously studied elsewhere abroad. They usually have spouses and families in China, as do those in the mid-group. Most of them already have career positions in China and are here to enhance their training. The mid-group struggled to pursue its education during the period of the government's unreasonable anti-intellectual bias and closing of schools. The younger group grew up with more educational opportunities and a more positive view toward Western culture and free enterprise. These students are more likely to be privately funded, single, and have fewer ties to their homeland. More of this latter group are likely to remain in the U.S.

The older the scholar the more he would have been exposed to Marxism. The younger the student, the more he may tend to be a pragmatic materialist without strong political convictions. Statistics show that over 95 percent of students and scholars coming from China today are irreligious with only a thin facade of Marxism. For many, private faith in Maoist tenets was rejected years ago. Confidence in the present hard-line regime was abandoned by most after the Tiananmen massacre. Many are searching for the truth and a credible world view, while others are disillusioned, wounded, cynical, even giving up hope in any belief system. They are following the same path that characterizes the post-Christian West.

At the same time, of all international students, Mainland Chinese are said to be the most open to Christian overtures and the gospel message. *God must have a plan for them!*

Struggles to faith

Confronted with Christianity, China's students and scholars wrestle with many problems and questions—political, philosophical, ethical, scientific, and cultural. They must reconcile their background in atheism and evolution and what seems to them to be a conflict between the Bible and science. They struggle with the meaning of life, immortality, moral standards, and the materialism and immorality they see in what they presumed was a Christian country.

Most intellectuals within China and those in the outside world are sincerely concerned with rebuilding a new China. They come from a background of strong nationalism, of putting the welfare of the state ahead of personal concerns. Pragmatically, they are exploring Western systems and economic philosophies to find what can benefit China. We Americans tend to be so individualistic that we take for granted everyone else considers personal advancement and private prosperity as his priority. Even our political interests seem chiefly self-serving. Many of us are preoccupied with what will bring the greatest gain to ourselves and our families.

Christians in the West also have a tendency to view Christianity primarily as a private faith emphasizing personal salvation. Partly for this reason Christianity was perceived by the educated class in China as otherworldly and not interested in addressing the ills of society, the misuse of power, or political injustices. Today's Chinese intellectuals may doubt that Christianity has anything to contribute to the building of their country.

As Christians, we need to understand their national concerns and not belittle their patriotism for China. We can show them that the gospel *does* deal with social issues. In the Scriptures God has demonstrated His concern for justice and the condition of man. He heard and heeded the cry of oppressed people. Especially is this expressed through the prophets.

Jesus' estimate of the value of the individual, his regard for justice, condemnation of hypocrisy and misuse of power especially in the religious community is clear. Moreover, we can accurately represent biblical Christianity as offering a valid and vital alternative to Marxism. Christianity has a world view based on a just and powerful God who is involved in His creation—this present world system. But we should be careful not to confuse eternal Kingdom values with our democratic political system. Or with aspirations for this temporal world alone. More about that in the final chapter.

Since the Tiananmen episode, many Chinese intellectuals seem to have changed their assumption that human nature is inherently good and only needs nurture in the right direction. Older intellectuals already experienced the terror and injustice of their government during the "Cultural Revolution," but younger ones were possibly more idealistic and trusting. The inhumanity they all saw demonstrated in their Marxist leaders in the Tiananmen affair and the continued violation of human rights has now caused them to fear what the possession of political power can do. They are facing the fact that according to the 1991 United Nations Human Freedom Index, China is near the bottom of the list in respect to human rights. Only Libya and Iraq were lower than China. We need to admit before our China scholar friends that the capitalist system or *any* political or economic system in the world can be equally inhumane when governed by spiritually fallen leadership.

Faith is a spiritual process

Let us not look upon Chinese students and scholars as "projects" or "targets" for our evangelism. Our ministry among them must be personal, loving, caring, and spiritual. We should be concerned for each one's normalization of relationship with God his Creator, through

Christ, the Reconciler. Whenever one of our friends steps into the Good Shepherd's fold, we should not view him as another trophy "for our side." We must not be "spiritual scalp hunters." They will doubtless not be won for Christ collectively but one-by-one and over a period of time.

As Western Christians, we should not be impatient for results as we pursue redemptive relationships with our friends from China. It may take an extended period for a Chinese scholar to change his life-long world view and reconstruct a new one based on Christian truths. Or, in the case of younger students, to formulate a world view for the first time. Openly confessing their Christian faith seems to be a more serious step for them than for some of us in the West. Baptism is an especially significant act that they do not take lightly. They will pay a high price if they convert to Christianity and return to China to share Christ. Political pressures, family relationships, and occupational advancement are at stake.

Since coming to genuine faith may be a long process for Chinese scholars, brooded over by the Holy Spirit, we cannot hurry the growth of seeds we have planted. We should not pull at them anxiously to see if they are growing. We should continue to water them with prayer and love and let them bear fruit *in the fullness of God's time.*

Sometimes Western Christians become anxious because they do not feel qualified to initiate friendships with Chinese students and scholars. It is certainly unnecessary to be an intellectual giant or a seminary professor to have successful Christian encounters with them. We don't need to know all about Marxism-Leninism, Maoism, Dialectic and Historical Materialism, Evolutionism, or Economics. We don't need to be experts in Christian apologetics or systematic theology, or have a degree in counselling. A wealth of excellent material, books and other resources both in Chinese and English on topics of their interest or struggles are available to give them. The ministries I have listed in *The Back of the Book* stand ready to assist you.

Establishing natural friendship bridges is the best approach *any* Christian can make. Do the loving, the caring, and the serving. Point The Way, demonstrate by your life how The Way has affected your life. Live the Jesus Way—then get out of the way. God does the converting. Let us not be superficial in our friendships. Our Chinese friends are very perceptive. They will know whether or not we have their real interests at heart.

Beware of stereotyped evangelistic approaches. Hitting them

with a few Bible texts is not redemptive witness. A patronizing manner gives the impression that we are just doing them a favor, not accepting them as the equals they are. Let us learn to listen and not act superior or domineering by doing all the talking. The Holy Spirit's personalized guidance is the final word in providing us with wisdom, discernment, humility, and sensitivity for this cross-cultural witness. Our Chinese friends will soon sense if we are pushing Americanism and belittling anything foreign. Let's not be afraid to admit deficiencies in our culture and political system and appreciate the positive aspects of their culture.

Home-spun friendships

Does it shock you to realize that 4 out of 5 international students are never invited to an American home while studying in this country? Let us as Christians be sure to open *our* doors to them. This is not a ministry at arm's length—not "at your doorstep." Invite them *further*—into your heart. Include your Chinese friends in your normal family life and activities. Home-centered witness has proven more effective, relaxing, and acceptable to them than constantly pressing for church attendance and meetings, especially in initial contacts. Respond to their practical and felt needs. Help with their living situations, household matters, driving lessons, banking, shopping. Be available to answer their questions, to share unconditional, informal time with no "religious" strings attached.

Remember that their academic workload is heavy and they may be finding it stressful to use a foreign language both for study and communication. Don't be disappointed if your Chinese friends can't respond to all your friendship overtures. Don't drop them or feel that you have failed because you don't see any spiritual response. You may feel frustrated if you have just begun building a good friendship when the student transfers to another school at a distance. Follow through as well as you can, keep in touch if possible, and continue to pray for him. Some plant, some water, some reap. Be faithful as *a part* of God's Harvest Team.

We have a wonderful opportunity to exercise our American freedom of speech and freedom of religion to share a clear Christian message with thousands of Chinese students and scholars.

But let's be sure it's the RIGHT message! Read on. . . . O

25

Ambassadors—For *Christ,* Not America

As World Christians we have a message for the world. It is distinct from our own tradition, ethnic identity, culture, or political structure. As Christians, we sometimes confuse our culture and traditions with Kingdom values.

When we travel, work, or minister abroad in secular or Christian capacities, we carry with us the baggage of our background, culture, and national experience. Sometimes deliberately, sometimes unintentionally, we tend to impose our cultural values and societal characteristics upon others. Missionaries of past generations inadvertently conveyed a blurred message, tainted with tradition and their particular brand of civilization. In China that contributed to Christianity being branded as "foreign" and "Western," although its roots were in the East.

We can easily fall into the same trap when we travel in China as tourists, when we serve in China as Christian professionals, and when we build friendship bridges with Chinese students and scholars in our own country. We are in danger of delivering a mixed message. As Christians, we are not called to be ambassadors for the United States (or any other country). We are "ambassadors *for Christ.*" We have an unique message that is distinct from that of the average secular American.

Examining our message

What is our message? Should we push freedom? Or democracy? Or capitalism and private enterprise? Human rights issues? Even freedom of religion? Are we to champion the superiority of our

American two-party government on the Jeffersonian model with caucuses, campaigns, primaries, and voting booths? These are not the Christian message.

We are justifiably proud and thankful to God that we live in a democratic country. We are far better off than if we lived in a totalitarian state where human rights are violated and atheism is a basic premise. We are happy to be Americans (or citizens of whatever countries my readers represent), no matter what our ancestral ethnic roots are. We cherish and enjoy our American liberties. But as Christians, we are not called by God to propagate these wonderful things mixed into our Christian message. If China eventually achieves a greater degree of political and personal freedom for its people, it may not, and probably should not, be exactly parallel to Uncle Sam's. After all, democracy in the American model is a johnny-come-lately in the history of world governments. Many countries, China included, use the word *democracy* but it does not necessarily mean to them what it means to us.

When the student demonstrators built the ill-fated "goddess of liberty" in Tiananmen Square, it was not a clone of our Statue of Liberty. It had distinct Chinese characteristics and meant something different to them than our symbol in New York harbor. We are thankful that America was founded on Christian principles. Our Constitution is a masterpiece designed to guarantee freedoms and we are proud of it. But our political system is not a suit of clothes that can fit *every* nation comfortably. True liberty and total freedom come only from Christ who said, "You shall know the truth, and the *truth shall make you free . . . I am. . .the Truth. . .*" (John 8:32; 14:6 NASB).

Our Bill of Rights is a superb document. We treasure it. But are its tenets essential for successful world evangelism? China's great explosion of Christian faith is happening in a repressive society without most of the "rights" and freedoms and conditions we consider necessary to spread the gospel.

Man's spiritual problems and the biblical solutions are the same regardless of what political system is in place. Democracy, private enterprise, human rights, and statues of liberty are not the *Christian* message for China, Czechoslovakia, Angola, or Argentina. A Christian world view cuts straight across all human institutions and structures.

To *serve the people* and work for the benefit of the state (Communism) is not God's highest plan.

To *serve yourself* with personal gain as priority (capitalism) is basically self-centered.

To *serve God* is the only WAY, TRUTH, and LIFE (the Christian message). That *leads* us to be concerned for our fellow men and our country. "But seek first His kingdom and His righteousness; and all these things shall be added to you" (Matt. 6:33 NASB). When our Christian priorities are right, when *First things* are put first, we shall also be personally satisfied and our needs supplied.

The gospel in focus

As Americans, we are often prone to look upon the rest of the world with eyes that are blurred with our freedoms and consumerism. Perhaps our priorities are out-of-focus because of national pride. Can we be realistic and humble enough to admit that capitalism can *also* be purely materialistic and have no intrinsic religious connotations? Materialism is just as false a god whether it wears a Mao cap, the stars-and-stripes top hat of Uncle Sam, or a French beret. Citizens of a democracy can be just as atheistic as Communists. In America the current slide into secular humanism and the growing anti-Christian bias in the media, in society, and in education is coming dangerously close to repressing some of the freedoms we have taken for granted. It depends on whose hands are at the power controls. Spiritual and moral values can drain to the same low level of corruption under *any* political order. There will not be a "Christian" political system until Christ comes in person to establish His Kingdom and reign on earth.

Without anchors in God, people in free, democratic nations are running wild, breaking laws, stealing from each other, murdering at random, and violating the rights of others. Liberty without the moral control that comes from the Judeo-Christian message can lead to license, laxity, licentiousness, and moral decay. The work ethic of many has declined in America. Too many are bowing down to false idols, gods made with hands, whether their names are Cadillac, IBM, or Sony. Multitudes are dabbling in the occult, and wasting their minds on drugs.

Without anchors in God, China's people, too, whether under totalitarian Marxism, pragmatic socialism, or some form of workable democracy for their unique situation will predictably go down the same road. Many of China's people have already lost faith in Communism, although they may be forced to mouth Marxist revolutionary slogans once again. Even their short-term experiment with limited capitalism under Deng's reforms seems to have left many feeling empty as deflated balloons. They need *the Christian message, not a political message.*

A young Chinese Christian demonstrating at Tiananmen was quoted in *News Network International,*

> China's students are not only calling for democracy. Underneath they are crying for real meaning in life. The materialism offered by Deng Xiaoping and his cohorts has backfired. People are starting to ask, 'Is this all we have to live for—a bigger television or a better refrigerator?' Chinese people need something more important to live for. We are not natural materialists. Now that Mao's vision is defunct and Deng's has been rejected, I am hopeful that many will come to Christ, whose vision is the greatest and most eternal in scope.

These young intellectuals from China are quick to observe *our* materialism. Our values are contagious. Do they watch us bow down to our idols of consumer goods—even in our Christian ranks? Is that what we have to share with them?

No "ism," including material*ism*, can provide ultimate satisfaction. Acquiring material goods will never fill the heart of the capitalist or the Communist. We become greedy, satiated, and feel barren and hollow. "Beware, and be on your guard against every form of greed; for not even when one has an abundance does his life consist of his possessions" (Luke 12:15), and "Man shall not live on bread alone" (Luke 4:4). Only the God of Abraham, Isaac, and Jacob, who entered our world system in the person of His Son, Jesus Christ, can fill every void and give meaning to life and death. "I came that they might have life, and might have it abundantly" (John 10:10 NASB).

In our close encounters of the Christian kind with Chinese people anywhere in the world will they clearly see Christian values reflected in our lifestyles? If not, our message is distorted.

Why offer substitutes or a counterfeit? We have *an authentic Kingdom message* to share with our Chinese friends. We have eternal *LIFE*, the true *LIGHT*, and genuine *FREEDOM* in Jesus Christ!O

The Back Of The Book

Chinese—An Easy Language?

The official language of China is Chinese. I'll bet you knew that! And did you know that the written form of the Chinese language is uniform throughout China? Anyone (a Chinese person, that is!) reading it silently can understand it no matter from what part of China he comes and regardless of what dialect he speaks.

But if he pronounces the characters (words), their pronunciation may be almost unintelligible to someone from another part of China—and they are both Chinese! The differences are far greater than what we think of as "dialects."

The official pronunciation recognized by China's government is Mandarin as spoken in the Beijing (Peking) area. It is also referred to as "putunghua." More than two-thirds of the Chinese people speak Mandarin; learning it is compulsary in schools throughout the land. In the Guangzhou (Canton) area of South China, people speak Cantonese as their primary dialect. Cantonese, or a variation of it, is what we most often hear spoken in the business communities of other countries because the majority of immigrants from China in the past were from South China.

Each ideograph is called a "character," which is an entire word with its own pronunciation, meaning, and tone. Each character must be memorized. The Chinese language in its character form has no alphabet so there is no spelling. Though it seems complicated to the Western mind, would you believe that until the mid-1700s more books were published in Chinese than in all the other languages of the world put together?

Through the centuries, however, only the elite, intellectual class of Chinese could read and write their own language because it took a lifetime to learn. The common people, the peasants who made up most of China's population, remained illiterate because of the difficulties of learning their own written language and because of their lack of opportunity to study.

Since the Communist government came to power in China, the Chinese written language went through major reforms to simplify the number of strokes that make up a character. This supposedly reduces the difficulties of learning. Most Chinese under age 40 use what is called the "simplified script." Many young people can also read the classic script but may have difficulty writing it.

Mind Your Z's And Q's

Let's have a mini-lesson in the Chinese language. You'll be glad you did if you travel to China. Chinese friends you meet in this country will also appreciate your efforts to pronounce their names and hometowns correctly.

Throughout this book and in China you'll come across the alphabetized version of the Chinese language as well as the Chinese characters. It is called "pinyin" and is based on the official Mandarin dialect. You will see it on China's street signs, buildings, in magazines, newspapers, etc. It is coming into more general use as China deals with the outside world. You won't have any problem getting used to it.

All vowels are enunciated and most of the alphabet letters have the same sound as English letters. Isn't that easy? There are a few important exceptions:

Q is pronounced like the ch in *ch*eer
X is pronounced like the sh in *sh*e
Z is pronounced like the ds in loa*ds*
C is pronounced like the ts in i*ts*
ZH is pronounced like the dg in ju*dg*e

These exceptions may seem strange at first, but there are only five of them. With a little practice on our "Who's Who?" list of names that follows, you will be able to pronounce Chinese acceptably. Where a previous system of spelling was in use, I have put that in parentheses the first time it appears. O

Who Is And Who Was
(At this writing)

Some of the names you may encounter in past and present happenings in China:

MAO ZEDONG (Mao Tse-tung): Notorious architect of Communist China and its revolutionary period. He was Chairman of the Communist Party and died in 1976.
CHOU ENLAI: Much loved Communist Premier of China, contemporary of Chairman Mao, who advocated a more moderate line toward the West. He died in 1976.

LIN BIAO (Lin Piao): Defense Minister during the "Cultural Revolution," and "ghost writer" of Mao's "Little Red Book" of revolutionary quotations. He was thought to have staged an abortive coup against Mao in 1971, fled for his life, and died in a mysterious plane crash. His name is linked with the "Gang of Four" in blame for many bloody crimes.

HUA GUOFENG (Hua Kuo-feng): Succeeded Mao as Chairman of the PRC for a short period.

HU YAOBANG: Succeeded Hua.

ZHAO ZIYANG: Succeeded Hu and was the former General Secretary of the Chinese Communist Party Central Committee, considered to be a reformist leader.

LI PENG: Premier of China.

JIANG ZEMIN: Former mayor of Shanghai, and Party Secretary.

YANG SHANGKUN: China's current President.

DENG XIAOPING (Teng Hsiao-p'ing): 88 year old former Senior Vice Premier of China, former Vice Chairman of the CCP, and former Chief of Staff who led the country in a drive toward modernization, prosperity, and relations with the outside world. He opened the way to a general consumerism. He emerged as China's No.1 strong man in 1978, was hailed "Man of the Year" by the U.S., but in the eyes of many became the "bad guy" after the bloody repression of democratic action at Tiananmen Square in 1989.

GANG OF FOUR: Included Jiang Qing (Chiang Ching) who was Mao's widow, and Wang Hungwen, Yao Wenyuan, and Zhang Chunqiao—the ultra-left clique within the Communist Party. They incited the heinous crimes of the "Cultural Revolution" and usurped much Party and State power. They were said to have influenced and used Mao in his declining years and plotted to seize control after Mao's death. Arrested shortly after their aborted coup.

SUN YAT-SEN: The professing Christian political leader of China who led the revolution which overthrew the Manchu dynasty and changed China into a Republic in 1911 after 3,600 years of dynastic rule. Sun was inaugurated as the first president of the Republic of China. Both the Communists and the Republic of China in Taiwan claim Sun Yat-sen as their "George Washington."

CHIANG KAI-SHEK: Generalissimo of the Nationalist Army and Kuomintang Party who was the leader of China during World War II. He fought unsuccessfully against the Communists and in 1949 went to Taiwan where he became the President of the Republic of China. ○

Glossary Of Terms Related To China

LIBERATION: A Communist term referring to 1949 when China came under the control of the Communist Party.

BOURGEOISIE: The capitalist class.

PROLETARIAT: The working class.

THE CULTURAL REVOLUTION: The lawless period of ten years, most extreme from 1966-76, officially called "The Great Proletarian Cultural Revolution." It was specifically directed at the elimination of the "Four Olds": old ideology, old customs, old habits, and old culture. Mao's wife was instrumental in this anarchist devastation and bloodshed. During this period, along with intellectuals and anyone connected to Western ways, China's Christians suffered imprisonment, banishment to labor camps, and death. Churches were closed and Bibles burned.

REVISIONISM: Modification of the "original" Marxist-Leninist philosophy and practice to suit new situations. China accused the former USSR of doing this and of losing the pure spirit of Communism.

THE FOUR MODERNIZATIONS: The modernizing of industry, agriculture, science-technology, and defense to develop China into a great, powerful, modern socialist country by the end of this century. Implemented by Deng Xiaoping.

TWO-LINE STRUGGLE: The socialist road versus the capitalist road.

THE LONG MARCH: In 1934-36 the 6,000 mile march from Jiangsi to Yenan by an army of courageous peasants and Communist soldiers. It was led by Chou Enlai and Mao Zedong.

PRC: The People's Republic of China.

ROC: The Republic of China (Taiwan).

CCP: The Chinese Communist Party

PLA: The People's Liberation Army.

POLITBURO: The small group of Communist leaders who form the powerhouse of China's government, the official decision makers.

RED GUARDS: Millions of China's youth, from school age through university, recruited by Mao to whip up revolutionary fervor. Mao gave them authority to devastate the country, destroy property and kill "enemies of the State" during the "Cultural Revolution." They wore red arm bands with the words "Hong Wei Bing" (Red Guards) and fanatically waved Mao's "Little Red Book." Ultimately Mao had to call on the Army to stop their out-of-control frenzy, and disperse them to the countryside to be reformed.

CADRES: Officials holding responsible positions in either the Party or the government and carry out grass-roots policies. Trusted persons indoctrinated in Communist ideology who, at lower levels, are not necessarily CCP members.

THREE-SELF PATRIOTIC MOVEMENT: (TSPM) China's political organization to control Protestant Christians. It exercises oversight of the registered churches and their activities. It is under the control of the Religious Affairs Bureau (RAB) which, in turn, is controlled by the United Front Work Department (UFWD), which is answerable to the Communist Party.

HOUSE CHURCHES or HOUSE GATHERINGS: Independent home meetings of China's Christians who do not wish to align themselves with the TSPM.

LITTLE FLOCK: An indigenous church group founded by Watchman Nee (Nee To-sheng) with which many house churches are still associated.

DIASPORA: Originally referring to the Jews who scattered to countries outside of Palestine after the Babylonian captivity. The term is commonly used to refer to the scattering of any people from their homeland to other countries. The Chinese diaspora refers to Chinese living outside of China. O

Sources And Resources

Newspapers And Periodicals Referred To
Or Quoted In The Text

(Any omission of credits or permissions is unintentional.
The author requests notification for future editions.)

Sources inside China

Amity News Service
Ban Yue Tan (Fortnightly Forum)
Beijing Review
China Daily
China Reconstructs (Renamed: *China Today*)
China Women's News
Gongren Ribao (Workers' Daily)
Guangming Ribao (Guangming Daily)
Interim Regulations on Private Enterprises for the PRC
Jingji Ribao (Economic Daily)
Jingjixue Zhoubao (Economic Weekly)
Liao Wang (Outlook Weekly)
Lilun Xinxi Bao
Renmin Ribao (People's Daily)
Xinhua
Zhongguo Qingnian Bao (China Youth News)

Sources outside of China

Asian Report. Hong Kong: Asian Outreach International
China and the Church Today. Hong Kong: Chinese Church Research
Center
China Educational Exchange Update. Harrisonburg: Mennonite Agencies
and Colleges.
China Horizon Magazine. Chicago: China Horizon, Inc.
China Insight. Colorado: OMF China Program
China News and Church Report. Hong Kong: Chinese Church Research
Center

News Network International. Santa Ana: Syndicate.
Pray for China. Hong Kong: Christian Communications Ltd.
Pray for China Fellowship. Hong Kong: Overseas Missionary Fellowship.
South China Morning Post. Hong Kong.
World Evangelization. Pasadena:Lausanne Committee for World Evange-
lization. ○

Note

(The resources and agencies, Christian and general, cited on the following pages are worthy of research, but their inclusion does not necessarily imply endorsement. Nor are they intended to be exhaustive. Newsletters or periodicals are available from many of the organizations.)

Books And Resources Related To China

Adeney, David H. *China: Christian Students Face the Revolution.*
Downers Grove: InterVarsity Press, 1973.
_____. *China: The Church's Long March.* Ventura and Singapore:
Regal Books and Overseas Missionary Fellowship, 1985. (Also in
Korean, French, German and Chinese editions)
Bloodworth, Dennis. *The Messiah and the Mandarins—Mao and the
Ironies of Power.* New York: Atheneum, 1982.
Bonavia, David, *The Chinese,* New York: Lippincott & Crowell, 1980.
Brown, Thompson G., *Christianity in the People's Republic of China,*
Atlanta: John Knox Press, 1986.
Bush, Richard C., *Religion in Communist China.* New York: Abingdon
Press, 1970.
Butterfield, Fox, *China: Alive in the Bitter Sea,* New York: Times Books,
1982.
Chao, Jonathan, ed., *The China Mission Handbook.* Hong Kong: Chinese
Church Research Center, 1989.
_____. *Wise as Serpents, Harmless as Doves: Chinese Christians Tell
Their Stories.* Pasadena: William Carey Library, 1988.
China Awareness Seminars, Littleton: Overseas Missionary Fellowship
China and Chinese Ministry, (Manual and Tape Series) C. Isaac Tam,
Editor, Wheaton: Institute for Chinese Studies, Billy Graham Center,
Wheaton College, 1988.
Christianity and China:Issues in Missions and Church History, (Manual
and Tape Series) C. Isaac Tam, Editor, Wheaton: Institute for Chinese
Studies, Billy Graham Center, Wheaton College, 1991.

Covell, Ralph. *Confucius, the Buddha and Christ*. Maryknoll, New York: Orbis Books, 1986.

Evangelical Perspectives on China. Edited by Donald E. Douglas. Farmington: Evangelical China Committee, 1976.

Ethnic Chinese Congress on World Evangelization CCCOWE. Sharon Wai-man Chan, Editor, Hong Kong: Chinese Coordination Centre of World Evangelism, 1986.

Francis, Lesley, *Winds of Change in China: Guidelines for Effective Service*. Singapore: OMF, 1985.

Gates, Alan F. *Think China*. Pasadena: William Carey Library, 1979.

Hamrin, Carol Lee, *China and the Challenge of the Future: Changing Political Patterns*. Boulder: Westview Press, 1990.

Johnson, David. *A Reasoned Look at Asian Religions*.

Kane, J. Herbert. *Winds of Change in the Christian Mission*. Chicago: Moody Press, 1973.

Kauffman, Paul E., *China, the Emerging Challenge: A Christian Perspective*, Grand Rapids: Baker, 1982.

Lambert, Tony, *The Resurrection of the Chinese Church*. London: Hodder & Stoughton and Overseas Missionary Fellowship, 1991.

Latourette, Kenneth Scott, *A History of Christian Missions in China*. New York: Russell & Russell, reissued 1967 (first published 1929).

_____. *A History of the Expansion of Christianity*, Vol.7, Advance Through Storm, New York: Harper & Brothers, 1945.

_____. *The Chinese, Their History and Culture*, 3rd ed., New York: Macmillan, 1961.

Lawrence, Carl, *The Church in China: How It Survives and Prospers Under Communism*. Minneapolis, Bethany House, 1985.

Lyall, Leslie, *God Reigns in China*. London: Hodder and Stoughton, 1985.

McInnis, Donald E., *Religious Policy and Practice in Communist China: A Documentary History*. London: Hodder and Stoughton, 1967, 1972.

Morton, W. Scott. *China: Its History and Culture*. New York: Lippincott & Crowell, 1980.

Mosher, Steven W. *Broken Earth: the Rural Chinese*. New York: The Free Press, 1983.

Neill, Stephen, *Colonialism and Christian Missions*, New York: McGraw-Hill, 1966.

_____. *A History of Christian Missions*. Harmondsworth: Penguin Books, 1964.

Paterson, Ross. *Heartcry for China*. London: Sovereign World Intl., 1989.

Patterson, George N., *Christianity in Communist China*. Waco and London: Word Books, 1969.

Schell, Orville. *In the People's Republic*. New York: Random House, 1977.

_____. *Discos and Democracy: China in the Throes of Reform*. New York:Doubleday, 1989.

Terrill, Ross, ed. *The China Difference: A Portrait of Life Today Inside the Country of One Billion*, New York: Harper Colophon, 1979.

_____. *Mao*, New York: Harper Colophon, 1980.

_____. *The Future of China After Mao*. New York: Dell Publishing Co., 1978.

Towery, Britt E., *The Churches of China*. Waco: Long Dragon, 1987.

Troutman, Charles. *Everything You Wanted to Know About the Mission Field But Were Afraid You Won't Learn until You Get There*. Downers Grove: InterVarsity, 1976.

Yang, C.K. *Religion in Chinese Society*. Berkeley: University of California Press, 1970.

Agencies For Professional Service Opportunities In China

Assist, P.O. Box 3370, Kent, WA 98032.

Career Impact Ministries, 711 Stadium Dr. E. Suite 200, Arlington, TX 76011.

Educational Resources & Referrals—China, 2606 Dwight Way, Berkeley, CA 94704-3000.

Educational Services International, Inc. 1641 W. Main St., Suite 401, Alhambra, CA 91801.

English Language Institute/China, P.O. Box 265, San Dimas, CA 91773.

Foreign Experts Bureau of the State Council, P.O. Box 300, Beijing, PRC.

Global Opportunities, 1600 E. Elizabeth St. Pasadena, CA 91106.

Global Resources Organization Ltd., P.O. Box 33608, Seattle, WA 98133.

Intercristo, 19303 Fremont Ave. N., Seattle, WA 98133.

Jensco Ltd., GPO Box 1987, Hong Kong.

Jian Hua Foundation, Flat A, 9/F., Hyde Centre, 221-223 Gloucester Rd. Hong Kong.

National Committee on United States-China Relations, 777 United Nations Plaza, New York, NY 10017-3521.

Overseas Academic Opportunities, 949 East 29th St. Brooklyn, NY 11210.

Overseas Missionary Fellowship China Program, 10 West Dry Creek Circle, Littleton, CO 80120-4413.

Peace Corps Recruiting Office, P.O. Box 638, Dallas, TX 75221.

Professional and Educational Services Intl. Inc., 8940 Reseda Blvd. Suite 103, Northridge, CA 91324

Professionals International, P.O. Box 27, Herndon, VA 22070.

235

Serve Asia Department: OMF, (Short term) 10 West Dry Creek Circle, Littleton, CO 80120-4413

Strategic Ventures Network, 1605 Elizabeth St. Pasadena, CA 91104.

Teachers For China, 2169 E. Monroe Terrace, Springfield, MO 65802.

University Language Services, P.O. Box 701984, Tulsa, OK 74170.

U.S. Association for Tentmakers, P.O. Box 919 Oak Park, IL 60303-0919.

WorldTeach, Phillips Brooks House, Harvard University, Cambridge, MA 02138.

(Some denominations have their own programs for professional service in China)

Books And Resources Related To
Christian Professional Service Overseas

Turner-Gottschang, Karen, with Linda A. Reed. *China Bound. A Guide to Academic Life and Work in the PRC.* Washington, D.C.: National Academy Press, 1987

Donovan, Katherine C., *Assisting Students and Scholars from the People's Republic of China: A Handbook for Community Groups.* Washington, D.C., CSCPRC and National Assn. for Foreign Student Affairs, 1981.

Forget the Pith Helmet: Perspectives on the Missionary Experience, Edited by Doug Wicks, Chicago: Moody Press, 1984.

Garrison, V. David. *The Nonresidential Missionary: A New Strategy and the People it Serves*, Monrovia: MARC, 1990.

A Guide to Living, Studying, and Working in the People's Republic of China and Hong Kong. New Haven: Yale China Assoc., 1986.

Hamilton, Don. *Tentmakers Speak*, Ventura: Regal Books, 1987.

Living in China: A Guide to Teaching and Studying in China, Including Taiwan. Rebecca Weiner, Margaret Murphy, Albert Li, San Francisco: China Books and Periodicals, 1991.

Loss, Myron. *Culture Shock: Dealing With Stress in Cross-Cultural Living*, Winona Lake: Light and Life Press, 1983.

Pierce, Elenor R. *All You Need to Know About Living Abroad.* Garden City: Doubleday.

Seamands, J.T. *Tell it Well: Communicating the Gospel Across Cultures*, Kansas City: Beacon Hill Press, 1981.

Study in China: A Guide for Foreign Students. Edited by Foreign Student Admin. Society, Beijing Institutions of Higher Education. Beijing: Beijing Languages Institute Press, 1987.

Wilson, J. Christy Jr. *Today's Tentmakers*, Wheaton: Tyndale House, 1979.

Yamamori, Tetsunao. *God's New Envoys.* Portland: Multnomah Press, 1987.

Ministries Among International Students

(Including or specifically among Chinese students and scholars)

Access, % Asian Outreach, P.O. Box 9000 Mission Viejo, CA 92690

Ambassadors For Christ, Inc. P.O. Box 280, Paradise, PA 17562

Association of Christian Ministries to Internationals, 7 Switchbud Pl. C 192-209, The Woodlands, TX 77380

Campus Crusade for Christ Intl, 100 Sunport Lane, Orlando, FL 32809-7875

China Horizon, P.O. Box 166053, Chicago, IL 60616-6053

China Institute, 1942 Michael Pl. Charlottesville, VA 22901

China Program:OMF, 10 West Dry Creek Circle, Littleton, CO 80120-4413

Chinese Christian Mission, 1269 N. McDowell Blvd., Petaluma, CA 94954

Chinese Ministries Division, Christian Aid Mission, 3045 Ivy Rd, Charlottesville, VA 22903

Chinese Overseas Christian Mission, Inc., P.O. Box 310, Fairfax, VA 22030

Christ Center Ministries, 4365 Telegraph Rd., Elkton, MD 21921

International Ministries Fellowship, 134 Miramar Dr. Colorado Springs, CO 80906

International Students, Inc., P.O. Box C, Colorado Springs, CO 80901

International Student Ministries, % InterVarsity Christian Fellowship, 6400 Schroeder Rd. P.O. Box 7895, Madison, WI 53707

The Institute of Chinese Studies, 1605 Elizabeth St. Pasadena, CA 91104

Mainland China Mission International, P.O. Box 487, Montgomeryville, PA 18936

The Navigators, P.O. Box 6000, Colorado Springs, CO 80934

People of the World, 2509 N. Granada St., Arlington, VA 22207

(Some denominations have their own ministries among international students)

Books Related To Chinese Students And Scholars Abroad

Beiler, Stacey and Dick Andrews. *China at Your Doorstep, Christian Friendships with Mainland Chinese*, Downers Grove: InterVarsity Press, 1987.

The Church's International Ministry. The Church's Outreach to International Students, Coordinator's Handbook, Colorado Springs: International Students, Inc. 1986

Lau, Lawson. *The World at Your Doorstep*, A Handbook for International Student Ministry, Downers Grove: InterVarsity Press, 1984.

Liu Zongren. *Two Years in the Melting Pot*, San Francisco: China Books & Periodicals, 1984.

Mainland Chinese in America—An Emerging Kinship. Edited by Edwin Su. Paradise: Ambassadors For Christ, Inc., 1991.

Morrison, Peter. *Making Friends with Mainland Chinese Students, a Christian Approach*, Hong Kong: Christian Communications, Ltd., 1984.

Rawson, Katie. *Come Join the Family: Helping Mainland Chinese Students in the West Turn to God.* The Woodlands: ACMI.

Wenzhong Hu and Cornelius L. Grove. *Encountering the Chinese--A Guide for Americans.* Yarmouth: Intercultural Press, 1991 .

White, Jerry and Mary. *Friends and Friendship*, Colorado Springs: NavPress, 1982.

Zhong, Joshua C.H. *Reaching Students from the People's Republic of China.* Colorado Springs: International Students, Inc. 1991.

Books Related To China Tourism

deKeijzer, Arne J., and F.M. Kaplan. *The China Guidebook.* Fairlawn: Eurasia Press, (current edition).

Fodor's People's Republic of China. Text by John Summerfield. New York: (current edition).

Samagaliski, Alan and Michael Buckley. *China—A Travel Survival Kit.* Australia: Lonely Planet Publ., 1991.

Schell, Orville. *Watch Out for the Foreign Guests—China Encounters the West.* New York: Pantheon Books, 1980.

Schwartz, Brian. *China Off the Beaten Track.* Hong Kong: St. Martins Press, 1983.

Christian Periodicals And Prayer Letters Related To China

Asian Report. Asian Outreach, P.O. Box 9000 Mission Viejo, CA 92690.

Bridge. Christian Study Centre on Chinese Religion and Culture, 6/F Kiu Kin Mansion, No.566, Nathan Rd. Kowloon, Hong Kong.

China and the Church Today. Chinese Church Research Center/China Ministries Intl. 1605 E. Elizabeth St. Pasadena, CA 91105.

China Broadcaster. F.E.B.C. Ltd. P.O. Box 96789, TST, Kowloon, Hong Kong.

China Educational Exchange Update, 1251 Virginia Ave., Harrisonburg, VA 22801.

China Horizon. P.O. Box 166053, Chicago, IL 60616-6053.

China News and Church Report. Chinese Church Research Centre, Box 312, Shatin P.O. N.T. Hong Kong.

China Notes. National Council of Churches, 475 Riverside Dr. New York, NY 10027.

China Prayer Update. Chinese Church Support Ministries, 2814 Rockhaven, Louisville, KY 40220

China Radio Flash. China Radio, P.O.Box 90, Shatin, N.T., Hong Kong.

Chinese Around the World. Chinese Coordination Centre of World Evangelism, P.O. Box 70189, Pasadena, CA 91117-7189.

Chinese World Pulse. Evangelical Missions Information Service, Box 794, Wheaton, IL 60187.

Christian Mission. 3045 Ivy Rd. Charlottesville, VA 22903.

Gospel Broadcaster. Far East Broadcasting Co. P.O. Box 1, La Mirada, CA 90637.

Pray for China. Christian Communications Ltd. P.O. Box 4293, Naperville, IL 60567-4293.

Pray for China Fellowship. OMF, 10 West Dry Creek Circle, Littleton, CO 80120-4413

Sky Waves. F.E.B.C. Chinese Ministries, P.O. Box 2016, Monterey Park, CA 91754-9909.

Voice of TWR. Trans World Radio (Far East), P.O. Box 98697 TST, Kowloon, Hong Kong.

Watchman on the Wall. Institute for Chinese Studies, 1605 E. Elizabeth St. Pasadena, CA 91104. O
